The Corporate Recruiter's Playbook

Strategies for Hiring Top Talent

Carmen Hudson

With Foreword by Jerry Crispin

The Corporate Recruiter's Playbook: Strategies for Hiring Top Talent

Printed in the United States of America.

To book Carmen Hudson for a speaking engagement or consulting services, please visit www.carmenhudson.com for additional information or send an email to carmen@carmenhudson.com.

Library of Congress Cataloging in Publication Data has been applied for.

For William

Foreword

I started my recruiting career in executive search as a researcher in the mid '90s, an early version of a sourcer. It was the dawn of the internet. One night I was working late, the General Manager found me in my cubicle and asked me to research a name he had scribbled on a scrap of paper. Before this interaction we'd only had a few conversations. Fifteen minutes later, I'd pulled together a dossier on the mystery person with as many details as I could collect, including address and phone number. If his raised eyebrows were any indication, the GM was impressed with my research. In fact, I think I frightened him a bit.

I loved that job - identifying potential candidates for our clients' mid- senior- level positions (what we called "name gen") and occasional functional or industry reports; I loved the transactional satisfaction of finding what was needed. Since my time at the executive search firm, sourcing has evolved from its transactional roots. These days, good sourcers are pulled into work that includes deep market research, outreach and attraction strategy, technology implementation, digital marketing and content creation. I have sourcer friends who have such advanced skills that their employers ask them to help select new market locations or evaluate new business opportunities.

As our methods and tools become more sophisticated, I believe that sourcing will become more than providing potential candidates as a need arises. Sourcers' ability to synthesize data and provide insight into talent markets could also help organizations *proactively* develop talent strategies.

Ahead of need, to support business initiatives and growth. I imagine that we will see the rise of sourcing pros who combine tactical search skills, data aggregation and recruitment marketing experience to advise and guide broader talent strategies. That's a job, were it available back in the 90s, I would have loved even more!

As it tends to happen, I went from sourcer to recruiter rather quickly. In fact, I was hired by Amazon as a sourcer (perhaps its first sourcer) but within months I found myself recruiting, then leading a recruiting team. The need was urgent. One day I found two employees alone in an office near mine. They had been saved from a lay-off from Amazon's Seattle distribution center, yet no one had shared their new assignment. I asked around, and no one knew who they were, or why they were there. Could I train them to source candidates for my positions? Someone told me yes.

Less than a year into my work at Amazon, I became a manager. I remember this happened in a hallway. My manager, who was then director, and later VP, asked me if this was something I wanted to do. I don't know that I'd thought much about it, but I said yes when the opportunity was offered. This was sometime in 2001, when things weren't so formal at Amazon. I can't imagine this happening today, but if you're ever offered the opportunity to advance your career in a hallway, say yes.

I was there about 3.5 years, but I learned so much. Things moved at a breathtaking rate. I learned the foundation of what I will share in this book at Amazon. Back then it was a laboratory. No one chastised you for making a change or taking a risk. You only got into trouble if you got it wrong and didn't move fast enough to correct your mistake. To this day, I thank John Vlastelica, Jeremy Eskenazi, Rick Dalzell,Scott Pitasky and many many others for making me a better recruiter, either for indulging my experiments or telling me when I got it wrong. It's the only way to get better – to feel safe enough to make mistakes, and to know that your mistakes will be corrected or redirected before you blow things up!

Since my time at Amazon, I've watched the profession shift and grow, and change, and demand more – greater investment, more respect, deeper understanding – from its practitioners and beneficiaries. Talent Acquisition sits at the center of modern organizations. More is demanded of us when things are going well. And even more is demanded of us when things aren't going well. It's never been a well-respected profession, and I doubt that it ever will be. It would be cool to see a recruiter rise from the ashes to become CEO, but I don't yet have an example of this from a major organization.

The purpose of this book is to house everything that I've learned in one place. You might use it as a jumping off place as you start or build your career in TA. I'd love to see others write similar tales until we get it right, until we harness all the information that makes us good recruiters into one big textbook, that we teach in universities (I have at least one buddy working on that as I write!).

Until then, I'm happy to share what I know, what I've learned about hiring top talent in some of the most revered organizations in the world. The intent of this book is to help you, the recruiter, the manager, the leader, develop a solid recruiting organization within a corporate setting. It is my hope that you read through this and think, *"great, I think I have the basics mastered and I learned a few things."* This book is written from the perspective of corporate recruiting, but those who work in third-party recruiting might find it helpful, or at least interesting. I've worked in third party agencies, but the bulk of my career has been in corporate, so that's where I'm placing emphasis.

Perhaps you are new at leading a recruiting team, or this is the first recruiting org that you've built. Perhaps you've always done things a certain way and you know that now is the time for change. Maybe you've got part of this right, but you know that there is room for improvement in other areas. I will share everything that I know (and a few things that I don't know but believe to my core). Perhaps you're managing a growing team and you want to see if you can gain some best practices and shave a few hours off the process. Take from this what is useful and drop anything that I recommend that doesn't work in your organization.

I don't think that I have written a great tome full of wisdom. I'm attempting to put into one place everything I can think of that will make your recruiting org hum, perhaps even succeed well beyond expectations. It is my sincere hope that someone comes along with a better book, with more advice on how to build a successful recruiting operation, even faster. It is my hope that this is only one drop in a big bucket of recruiting effectiveness.

Before you start this book. Grab a yellow legal pad and as you read along, make a habit of jotting down areas you'd like to change or address in your organization. I'd love to see your list. When you finish reading, send me the list of stuff you'd like to tackle. I think it would be interesting to see where the lists intersect! My email address is carmen@carmenhudson.com.

Forward by Gerry Crispin

Life-long Student Nurturing a Community of TA Leaders

What you will find in Carmen Hudson's The Corporate Recruiter's Handbook: A Comprehensive Guide to Hiring Top Talent is a pathway to ownership and leadership of the most critical business function -- the hiring process.

Recruiters are arguably the tip of the HR spear. If we do our job as well as we are expected to, then our HR colleagues will have little to do (although whenever I say that it is a bit like poking the bear. Still, I believe it).

Carmen has hit the triple play by sharing her extensive experience, knowledge and skills as a practitioner, consultant, and teacher with some of our country's most iconic employers. Learn from it and you will not only yearn for more, you will be sharing your own insights as you recognize you've joined a unique community evolving our way forward.

This guide may be positioned as a 'handbook,' but each line is imbued with personal stories, reflections, logic, data and insights on how to own the function, take pride in our profession and support our firm's corporate values.

I especially love the fact that Carmen begins with the most vulnerable stakeholder and, in the second half, dramatically expands the section on leadership. Compassion for the humans who express an interest in our firm, whether we go forward with them or not, must become core to our personal satisfaction as a professional and should never be compromised. And while everyone may not wish to become a leader, we all have a responsibility to exhibit leadership by stepping up to influence our peers and colleagues with the skills, knowledge, and experience (and data) we bring to work.

I am a firm believer that recruiting in the 21st century will require that we all agree to a comprehensive, yet basic body of knowledge- standards for how we treat each stakeholder as well as support the business necessity to populate our workforce with competent and motivated employees.

To achieve that goal however we need to up our game. If we took formal courses on subjects like Rewards & Compensation Theory, Staffing Organizations, Assessment and Selection, Organizational Transformation and much more, this handbook is their practical companion.

In fact, I took those courses (in the age of the dinosaurs) and, upon joining Johnson & Johnson as a young professional after 6 years of graduate education studying I/O psychology, I couldn't wait to develop award winning behaviorally anchored rating scales for every job, map and audit every decision at every step in a candidate's journey and create an internal programs to predictively validate our hiring decision processes.

Fortunately, an experienced recruiting manager took me under his wing and helped me see that before I went off half-cocked on what I believed we needed, I should immerse myself in the practical side of how we do what we do today. He pointed out that my desire to solve complicated problems didn't change the fact that the Hiring Manager (HM) I would be cutting my teeth on expected 3 quality candidates scheduled in 3-4 weeks. He had me:

a. Interview ½ a dozen candidates myself

b. schedule the 2nd best first.

c. schedule the best candidate 2nd

d. schedule the worst candidate 3rd

then, e) He wanted me to go in and review my take on the 3 candidates and get the HM to agree that the second candidate was the best and they only get worse from here on out. Finally, he said, "Then come back and see me."

Now don't get any wild ideas that the above is a worthwhile approach to hiring. The context I described is a world that no longer exists -- but there are two take-aways from my experience and the conversation with my new 'coach.'

The first is that at every recruiter should have a point of view in serving the goals of the function and a responsibility to step up and participate, even to influence in the context of the broader business needs, not necessarily the HM's need and, to learn how to do it constructively, logically and with data -always. But first and foremost is to understand where you are starting from and demonstrate you can do it well. Only then can you build a practical strategy to an end state and the trust of those you need to sell it to.

The second is about leadership - formal or not. Empowering your team and your teammates to work at building trust with every stakeholder in the process including (and especially) the candidate is an essential component of recruiting. We all have the capacity to provide leadership by virtue of our passion for the work, our compulsion to improve, our willingness to challenge constructively and share unconditionally.

The Corporate Recruiters Handbook: A Comprehensive Guide to Hiring Top Talent is not an academic tome. It is a companion piece that points to a path forward and serves up the tools to make your own way.

I'll end with this quote, as it describes best what Carmen Hudson has to offer:

> *"True teachers are those who use themselves as bridges over which they invite their students to cross; then, having facilitated their crossing, joyfully collapse, encouraging them to create their own."*

– Nikos Kazantzakis

Contents

Part I -
The Recruiter's World

You may be reading this as a line recruiter, or perhaps you are a leader looking for little inspiration. In either case, I don't think it's possible to be great without first mastering the basics. In my case, this took years – far longer than it should have – because recruiting knowledge was passed from mouth to mouth, experience to experience, without anyone writing it down. Without anyone providing a baseline from which to start. I'll share my thoughts on the overall recruiting process, how I think it should go, but I wouldn't rule out what works for you, your team, your corporate environment. You're there, in the hot seat. You know what your org needs, what it will and will not tolerate. You'll likely have to make a few tradeoffs. I get it. But if something's off, not going well, needs improvement, I'd return to your foundation and figure out if something is missing.

My underlying assumption is that, in most cases, just a few steps are missing to make a recruiting team go from OK to real corporate heroes. In some cases, those steps take place at the beginning of the process. In other cases, the middle gets cloudy, and some important steps get missed, or perhaps it is near the end where steps get skipped. Overall, this is what I think a basic recruiting process should look like:

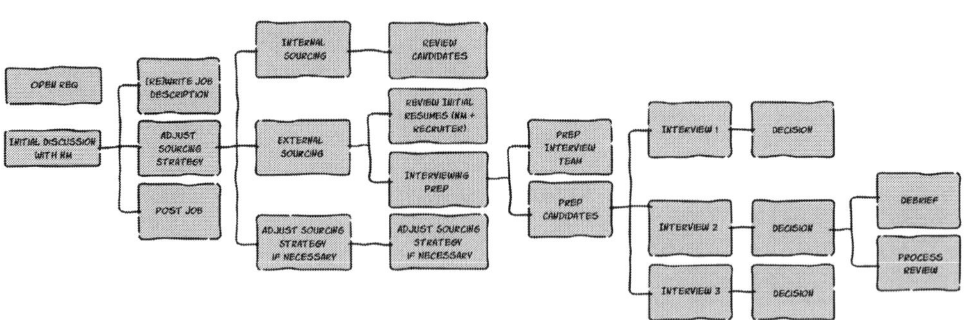

Illustration 1

This chart represents a broad outline of how the process has worked best for me, as a corporate recruiting leader. My guess is that had I tried to sketch out the process earlier in my career, I might have skipped some important steps. I'll try to cover all the elements in this chart, plus some of the unseen, uncharted bits of the recruiting process. Again, take from this that which works in your environment, drop what doesn't work after trying and add those steps I might have missed. And share. What makes you successful? The rest of us want to know!

Chapter 1 - The Candidate Experience

You've likely seen surveys, data and papers that extol the virtues of a great candidate experience, and I encourage you to digest all of it, and hold the candidate experience in an exalted position. In fact, I would change the candidate experience to "the Recruiting Experience" if I didn't fear that the term would lose all relation to reality.

Candidate experience, at its base, means that the candidate that interacts with your recruiting org, has an experience. You get to define how consistent that experience is, and what are the absolute promises that you make to candidates when they interact with recruiters, hiring managers and anyone (or anything) else that is part of the process. Going even further, you get to decide what, exactly, is a candidate. Are the people who complete online applications candidates? What about those who speak with recruiters or managers over the phone? What about the internal woman who raises her hand, albeit shyly, wondering if she has the required skills and knowledge to apply for the new role?

Candidates, if they could have it their way, wouldn't interview, wouldn't face any competition in the job-seeking process. I don't know this to be true, but I would place a heavy bet on the notion that the candidate experience (as defined by the candidate) declines as competition increases.

A senior, super rare engineer gets treated differently than a customer service representative. The two experiences should be different, to be sure, but the care and feeding that go into the design and execution of the process should be equal.

That said, our candidates' impression of what we do falls well below what we think we do! From the 2022 North American Candidate Experience Benchmark Report, we know that:

- Many companies still fail to follow up with applicants to let them know if they will be moving forward (or not) in the process – almost 40% of applicants reported no communication after applying

- Only 44% of candidates were informed about what would happen next, after interviews

- Many candidates do not perceive the process as fair, indicating that we need to do a better job of explaining the process to candidates

- Candidates favor a structured interview process; the highest rated CandE award winners with structured interview processes received higher positive ratings and were more willing to refer their friends

*I encourage you to read over the CandE research report (and participate in the annual survey) to better understand what practices appeal to candidates. You can find more information, as well as the free report here.

So what should comprise the candidate experience? How should we measure it to know that we met candidate expectations? Here's a gathering of what is commonly measured:

- How easy it is to search for and find a new position?

- How easy it is to use the job search and career pages on your corporate website?

- Are job descriptions easy to read and understand?

- Is the application process straightforward and easy to execute? Do you ask candidates to apply via LinkedIn, or submit a resume, only to lure them into your corporate application process asking them to provide resume details yet again? (Don't say no until you've audited this process yourself. You'd be surprised at how many companies require "double application")

- Do you respond/follow up in a timely way, at multiple points during interview process? The CandE's tell us that within five days is what candidates expect.

- How do candidates rate your phone screen and interview effectiveness?

- How fast are you able to make and communicate a decision?

- Offer alignment and communication

Here are some other areas that aren't commonly measured, but perhaps should be:

- Ability for candidate to provide feedback to recruiters and the interview team

- Interviewers prepared and aligned

- Frequency, speed and effectiveness of feedback and other communication from employer

I think it's important to consider each area of measurement and then figure out, in order of importance, which metrics you will use to measure success in your environment. From the candidate's point of view, response time and decision speed are likely the most critical areas. But as a recruiting team, candidate satisfaction is not the only lens through which we look at candidate experience. It may be even more important that candidates review and select the right job, so fixing issues related to job descriptions and job postings might be more important to you. The point is that you look at all available data, talk to your hiring managers, recruiters, HR partners and leadership to determine what needs fixing, urgently. Then run down your list systematically to ensure that your organization is treating candidates well.

I can tell you that, anecdotally, fixing candidate experience issues goes a long way toward enhancing your reputation and the reputation of your company. Get it right consistently, and the word spreads quickly. Treating candidates well is the easiest way to get high-quality referrals from past candidates.

So how do you, recruiter, develop good habits when it comes to keeping candidates happy? For me it came down to organizing communication. Monday – I checked my schedule, made a note of who I was scheduled to screen, who was coming in for an interview during the week, which hiring teams had interviews, and to which candidates I owed some sort of communication. I learned to check this schedule again a couple of times during the week. I scheduled my declines for Friday mornings or afternoons. For me, it was best do it all at once.

I also relied heavily on my recruiting coordinator, and tried to check in daily, giving a heads up if things were looking like they were going to get hairy. I have been so fortunate – many of the coordinators I worked with were anxious to become recruiters, so they were willing to take on anything I was willing to leave in their laps. I didn't ask them to manage candidate declines – I believed that was my responsibility as the recruiter – but they helped me with scheduling and kept me honest when it came to saying "no."

The key for me was to keep my promises. If I told a candidate that I would get back to them with a decision within a week, then I did that, or I had a conversation about why the decision had been delayed. I put myself in the shoes of the candidate, and I know that no one likes waiting around. Recruiting is rooted in speed. To quote Hyman Roth in *The Godfather*, "This is the business we've chosen."

TL;DR

- Read the CandE report to understand what candidates expect
- Response time and decision speed are most important to candidates
- Treating candidates well, and fixing any related issues, goes a long way toward enhancing your employer brand and your ability to hire top candidates
- Find a way to monitor your candidate activity and do everything you can to keep your promises

Chapter 2 – Getting Started with a Req

We're going to jump right in to where the action starts. There is a whole series of activities that happen before recruiting starts, but we'll save that for the Management section. Right now, you have a job to do!

You've been asked to recruit. A new software developer. A replacement for the marketing director that left for greener pastures. A new class of 5-6 customer service representatives. Doesn't matter the position, kick-off time is here. What follows is a checklist of recommended activities. Some are strongly recommended – I'll put those in bold. My list comes from years of experience. No one gave me this list when I started. This list is a result of trial and error. I'll share a few illustrative examples as I go along. But believe me, if you plan to be a trusted and successful corporate recruiter, if you plan to lead recruiters, mastering this list is the foundation of becoming a great recruiter. I learned the hard way.

1. **Get an appointment on the hiring manager's schedule.** This is important. Before you post the job, or take an action on the req, you need to know a bunch of stuff. Stuff you shouldn't guess or rely on the departmental scuttlebutt to discern. But that doesn't mean that you should wait until the manager's meeting to get started. Being a good recruiter requires that you move fast, that you're able to peer around corners, that you're able to anticipate the questions, able to see common pitfalls before hiring managers or candidates (or you) fall into the holes that await you.

2. Prepare for the HM kickoff meeting. Get the small stuff out of the way and settled. Review (and re-write) the job description. Get the appropriate sign-offs and req numbers. Post the job (you can change it if the description changes, but managers love it when they don't have to remind you to get the job posted!) **Learn about the hiring manager's team by reviewing their LinkedIn profiles.** Review the profiles of current and past holders of the job, both in the hiring manager's department, and in other departments.

3. The next thing I advise recruiters to do is to thoroughly understand the job requirements. **Diagram the job so that you have a basis for understanding the role.** Don't worry about being 100% correct. Your job is to walk into that meeting with the manager with some sort of understanding, versus starting with absolutely no clue. I started this practice when I was at Amazon, and technical roles were crushing me. One day, Amazon's first CTO wanted to make sure that my team was focused on hiring engineers for the "S3" business (the early name for Amazon's now well-known AWS – Amazon Web Services -- business). He spotted me and some others in a conference room, popped in, and emphasized the importance of hiring engineers for this group. Sensing that we had no idea what this group was about, he drew a diagram and explained what they were building. I still had little understanding of this business. But his drawing helped me better understand the type of candidate needed. From that point, I started diagramming jobs, using the technique I learned in grammar school to diagram sentences, to better understand the jobs for which I was recruiting. And it helped! Often, I got it wrong. But my hand-drawn diagrams were a good jumping off point. The diagrams helped me better understand the skills and qualities that were most important. The drawings gave my hiring managers a way of explaining the jobs in a manner I understood. Often, they were surprised that I understood as much as I did. And often, they were just as inarticulate about describing a job as I was, just in a different way. They knew the technical specs of the job, but they didn't know how to talk about the work in a way that would be appealing to candidates. The

diagrams gave us both a jumping off point and a quicker way to get to what we needed from each other.

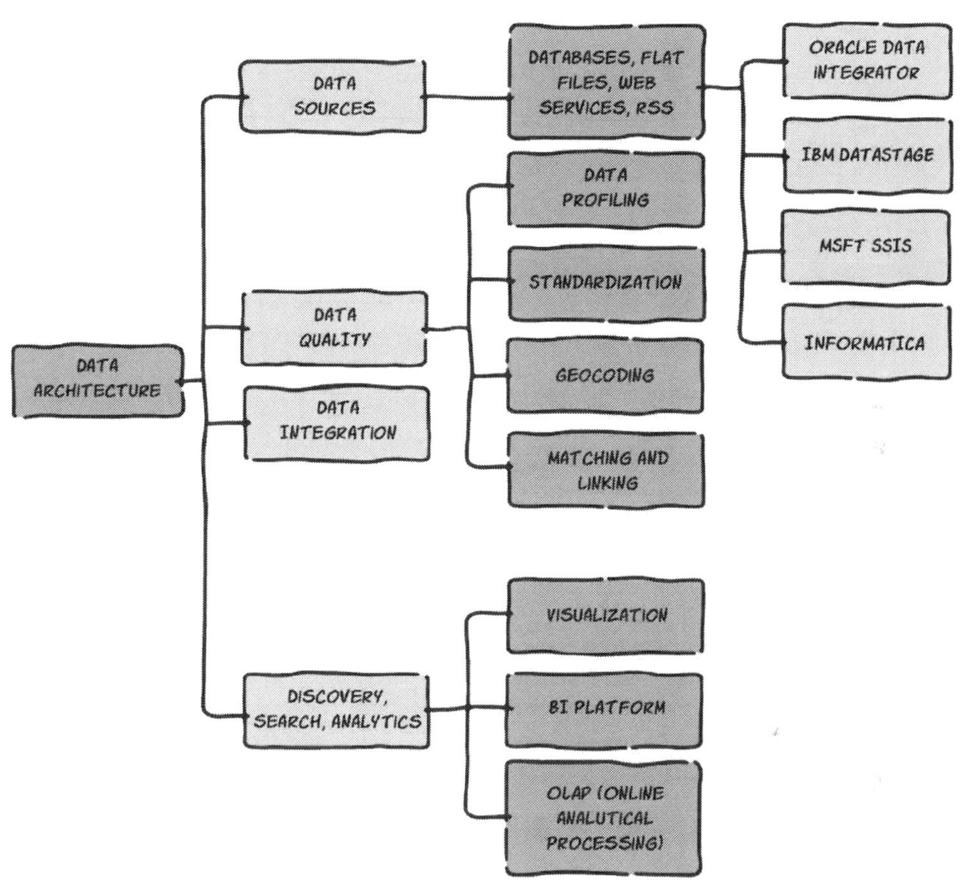

[Illustration 2 - Diagram of Software Architect, Data Platforms]

4. **Outline what you will do, and what you expect the hiring manager to do.** Recruiting requires a bunch of tugging and pulling, quite a bit of nudging and pushing and everything in between. You can't do it all. The best hiring managers know this and are willing to do everything necessary to get a hire as quickly as possible. Some managers despise recruiting and wish to shove it all off on you. Most fall somewhere in between, either they

don't know how they should contribute to the process, don't remember, or their work with an incompetent or under resourced recruiter left them with bad habits. Your job is to assess the manager's needs and communicate consistently every single time even if you've worked with the manager before. It's your consistency that is important. Not only will the manager know what to expect, their team will learn as well. That way as team members grow and become managers, they become fluent in the language of recruiting. Even if you never work with the team again, your reputation will precede you and prepare other managers for working together.

I've shared a couple of emails I like to fire off to managers before and after meeting to discuss the open position in the appendix. Reiterating in writing is an easy way to formalize the process and document what you commit to doing, and what you expect the hiring manager to contribute.

5. **Following your kickoff meeting, set regular and frequent update meetings.** Do this up front, put the meetings on the manager's calendar. For most roles 1x per week will get the job done. Some roles might require lesser frequency, others, especially if the timeline is compressed, might require more meetings. The quicker and more enthusiastically your manager agrees to meeting regularly, the greater chance you have of being successful. Getting this commitment is as much about gauging how important this hire is for the manager as it is about a smooth recruiting process. This is your first chance to assess if the manager has skin in the game.

6. **After the kickoff, write down what you will do, what you expect the manager to do and share the timeline.** Often recruiters will do everything to avoid committing to a timeline. "Recruiters don't control the outcome," I often hear. "We can't predict when we'll make a hire." I call bullshit. A CEO or sales leader cannot predict with 100% certainty whether or not customers will buy a product or not, yet they are expected to predict and hit sales targets every quarter. As the recruiter, it is not your job to become Merlin and magically produce a hire in two weeks when you know that the market has few candidates, the job is less than desirable, and the

pay is sub-standard. You know that it will take you three months to find the best candidate. The hiring manager, of course, wants the new hire in two weeks. If you don't have a conversation with the manager about market conditions, and a realistic timeline, he or she will assume that two weeks is enough time, and you will have failed when day 14 comes around. Commit to a timeline – in writing – and review it every week. Reserve the right to make changes as the process requires. If sourcing is more difficult than anticipated, or if you're delayed, renegotiate the timeline. If the most important interviewer goes on vacation, update and communicate the new timeline. Trust me, your honest assessment of the timeline and your ability to communicate the timeline with the hiring manager is perhaps your most important skill, and the easiest way to develop a reputation for doing good work. Pushing back on unrealistic timelines may first prove difficult or uncomfortable, but it is the mark of an experienced, honest recruiter. Once I mastered this skill, I slept better, feeling confident that I could achieve what I had promised. Before that, I could only hope to meet the accelerated expectations of uninformed hiring managers.

TL;DR

- Set up a time to meet with the manager but prepare before the meeting. Learn about the hiring manager and their team. Research the open position before the meeting, diagramming the position if that is helpful.

- After meeting with the manager, send an email outlining what you will each do and outlining the timeline.

- Set regular and frequent check-in meetings until the job is done!

Chapter 3 - Kicking off With Hiring Managers

Get this right early on and you will enjoy a long and successful recruiting career. I stumbled through this for quite a while before I figured out how to have a productive conversation with a hiring manager. There was no toolkit, no training class, no words of wisdom that helped me figure it out. I learned by trial and error.

And here is a secret. You will not collect all the information you need at the kick-off. It's only a start. There are many conversations that you will need to have to recruit successfully. The kickoff meeting sets you up to have those conversations, to begin to build the trust needed to foster a healthy recruiter/hiring manager relationship.

It's tempting to meet with the manager the moment the req is approved. He or she is likely anxious to get started. My advice is to schedule a kickoff (or strategy meeting, or whatever you call it, meeting right away. Just don't call it an intake meeting. "Intake" suggests a one-sided, order-taking, uneven relationship and does little to set you up for success). But give yourself some time to prepare for this meeting. As mentioned previously, learn as much as you can about the manager, the team and the job as time allows before the kickoff meeting. Your job is to show up with an assortment of answers and work with the hiring manager to select the right solutions. What level is the job? Within the level is the manager looking for someone with a higher level of skills to complement the existing team, or is he or she more attuned to compensation, and willing to train someone on the more advanced requirements of the job? If you have done your homework and can quickly confirm the basics of the job requirements, you can afford to use the time to understand the hiring manager's needs more deeply, and even challenge them if you think they aren't thinking about the role broadly (or narrowly) enough. Some things to make sure get covered:

1. Agreed upon target candidate profile (performance expectations, hiring criteria, level, target companies)

2. Aligned on target compensation (educate and align on compensation realities)

3. Discuss and agree upon sourcing and selling strategy (specific sourcing plan to be confirmed after the meeting if additional research on best sources or budget approval for additional sourcing cost is needed, update the job ad after the meeting if needed)

4. Discuss and agree upon interviewing strategy, process, interviewers (interviewing approach to be confirmed during or after the meeting)

5. Align on overall recruiting goals (slate of X interview-ready candidates by Y date), roles of Hiring Manager and Recruiter, timeline for overall process (expectation setting conversation)

You may not be able to cover all of this in your first meeting, especially, if it's only a half hour. Show the manager the list anyway and assure them that you will cover the topics in subsequent meetings. In fact, make sure you agree on a regular meeting cadence, and calendar a set of meetings that end one or two weeks after the candidate is hired. It is important that the manager understands that hiring is a short-term project that will need quite a bit of his or her, as well as your, attention over the next X weeks or months. It's very likely that they will make few decisions as important or as expensive as this one, and you're here to shepherd them through the process and help them make the best decisions.

A note to insert here. Make sure that you introduce yourself to the hiring manager. Make sure that they know your accomplishments in recruiting (or newness to the field) and share what you have learned about the manager and give them a chance to add a bit of color. You will be working together on one of the most expensive, important decisions they will make that week/month/year, and it's critical that you each have at least a baseline understanding of goals and accomplishments.

In the best-case scenario, you and the manager get along famously, you get down to agreement on the profile, the interview team, the sourcing strategy and all of the other details. In most cases, you will nail some of this, but will need subsequent meetings to deliver everything promised.

Follow up your first meeting with the hiring manager with a written summary of all you will do, all that the hiring manager will do, remind them of your meeting schedule, important dates and action items, and your next meeting.

See Item 3 in the appendix for an example of an email to send to the hiring manager after the kickoff meeting. Following up in writing assures the manager that you've thought deeply about the role, even if you didn't have time to cover a topic in your meeting. Additionally, a written record of what needs to be done, what to expect and timelines will be important down the line.

I'd be doing you a disservice if I stopped here, merely informing you of *what* you need to do to be successful. Your career as a recruiter will made or broken, based on your relationship with your hiring manager. *How you* accomplish your work is as important as what you do to get it done.

Hiring managers come in all shapes and sizes, all levels, and abilities, some very interested in recruiting, some with a palpable distaste for it. Your job is to figure out your manager's abilities and desire to recruit, and to help them fill in the blanks where possible, all in the name of making a hire. I've worked with hiring managers who were brand new to management and appreciated every tidbit I was able to share. I've also worked with managers who absolutely hated recruiting, hated me or both. I'm proud to say that I tried to give every manager my best. I managed to become friends with quite a few of them. I think I may have managed to change the minds of a few (recruiting isn't so bad, if done right). And I have disappointed a few managers. For that I am truly sorry. I always tried to do my best. And I learned, quickly, from my mistakes.

As I mentioned earlier, before you meet with your manager, try to learn a bit about them. Have they lead big teams before? Is this their first management role? When did they join the company? Why – what are they here to accomplish? The more you know, the better you will be able to find talent and help the manager and his or her team make quick, appropriate decisions.

Your job as the recruiter is to anticipate and remove roadblocks along the way. Be proactive. Get answers before you need them (if our current hot candidate rejects our offer, are we prepared to raise the salary or should we move on to the next candidate?). Be insistent on setting, resetting and meeting timelines. The name of the game is honesty. Some searches, because of market conditions and talent availability, cannot be wrapped up in a month. For the love of the industry, get comfortable talking about timelines and learn how to accurately predict, and set expectations around time-to-hire.

As you get comfortable working with a manager, developing a strong relationship, be sure to collect their views on TA. What could be done better? What do they think about making salaries public? What are they hearing within the industry that might be useful? These kinds of conversations not only strengthen your relationship and your knowledge; it is also the kind of information you want to gather as you move toward leadership.

It is important that you recognize your role as an advisor. When you have a conversation with a hiring manager about increasing salaries, share ideas about how to address the impending problem. Is it time to sit down with the comp team? Time to adjust the skill level on the team? Make those recommendations, lead the action and become a talent advisor, expand beyond the role of recruiter.

Sometimes, we get it wrong. We lose the perfect candidate to the competitor. We miss an important step, or we miss a due date. I can't tell you the number of times I've messed up, due to my own ineptitude or circumstances out of my control. As I got better at recognizing what could go wrong, and confident enough to speak up about impending problems, I was able to alert managers in advance, and began to develop a reputation of being a good recruiter. There were many times, however, that I didn't speak up, many instances in which I was surprised, times I didn't set a timeline, times I didn't meet the timeline. Important things I forgot. If we're ever in a bar together, and you buy me a really nice glass of red wine I might tell you about my biggest screw up ever. Let's just say that there is a difference between 500, 5,000 and 50,000 stock options.

What I eventually learned is that in this business, being upfront and transparent – even about my mistakes – was the best way to go. That, and learning a hard lesson once, not twice, is preferred.

The last bit of advice I might offer is to encourage the hiring manager to bring someone else on the team along. If the manager wants to do less work, and has a team member they are considering promoting, or developing, add that person to all conversations and activities. Recruiting well is a skill that all future leaders must build, and your hiring manager will likely appreciate the suggestion. Not to mention, you will have two people on the team dedicated to doing the work to fill the role.

TL;DR

- Spend a good amount of time preparing for the kickoff meeting with the hiring manager. Learn as much as you can about the team, the role, why the position is open, the manager's professional history. Prepare to have a targeted, in-depth conversation that leads to action and results.

- Set a timeline. You're not a talent advisor until you're able to set, manage and meet a reasonable timeline.

Chapter 4 – Sourcing and Screening

Often, hiring managers (or even recruiters) think of sourcing as synonymous with recruiting. It isn't. Recruiting involves a number of steps that we're outlining in this book. But sourcing well – quickly and efficiently – is an important part of the recruiting process. I know very few corporate recruiters who haven't learned at least one aspect of sourcing well. And I know plenty of recruiters and sourcers who think in Boolean logic and find immense pleasure in finding candidates outside of the ATS and LinkedIn. I love the complexity of a tough search, but I've also watched as my hiring manager beamed because I was able to unearth a referral candidate in record time. Find what works for the org you support and do that well. Share with others. Perhaps find another sourcing challenge and learn that, too.

We won't cover everything about how to source in this book – there are many references and online resources, and I'll list a few good books about sourcing at the end of this book. But I will share with you a few tricks that made sourcing the easiest, perhaps the most enjoyable part of the job for me.

The first thing you must do is iron out what you need to do to find suitable candidates for the role, and the length of time you think it will take, with your hiring manager. Secondly, the two of you should align on what this search requires, what's nice to have, what the hiring manager will and will not accept as a candidate.

I shared this earlier, but it might be worthwhile to take a deeper dive into my methodology. Early in my career I was faced with a lot of technical roles. I had very little knowledge of technology, and I often worked with newbie hiring managers who likely didn't understand my limitations. I also suspect that they had little hiring experience and little idea of the kind of language needed to attract a jobseeker. The managers were often consumed by what a good candidate could do. It took a bit of conversation to help them see that at this stage, we should also communicate the environment that the candidate will work in, why the candidate should be excited about the work and the organization. More senior hiring managers get this, but often, new hiring managers just haven't given much thought to what the job looks like from the jobseeker's point of view.

So, even if you know what you're looking for, it helps to draw it out for the manager. Do this in advance (or know how you would draw and label the position in advance. I did this once for a hiring manager, in the moment, at Microsoft and she thought I could walk on water!)

First, the job description:

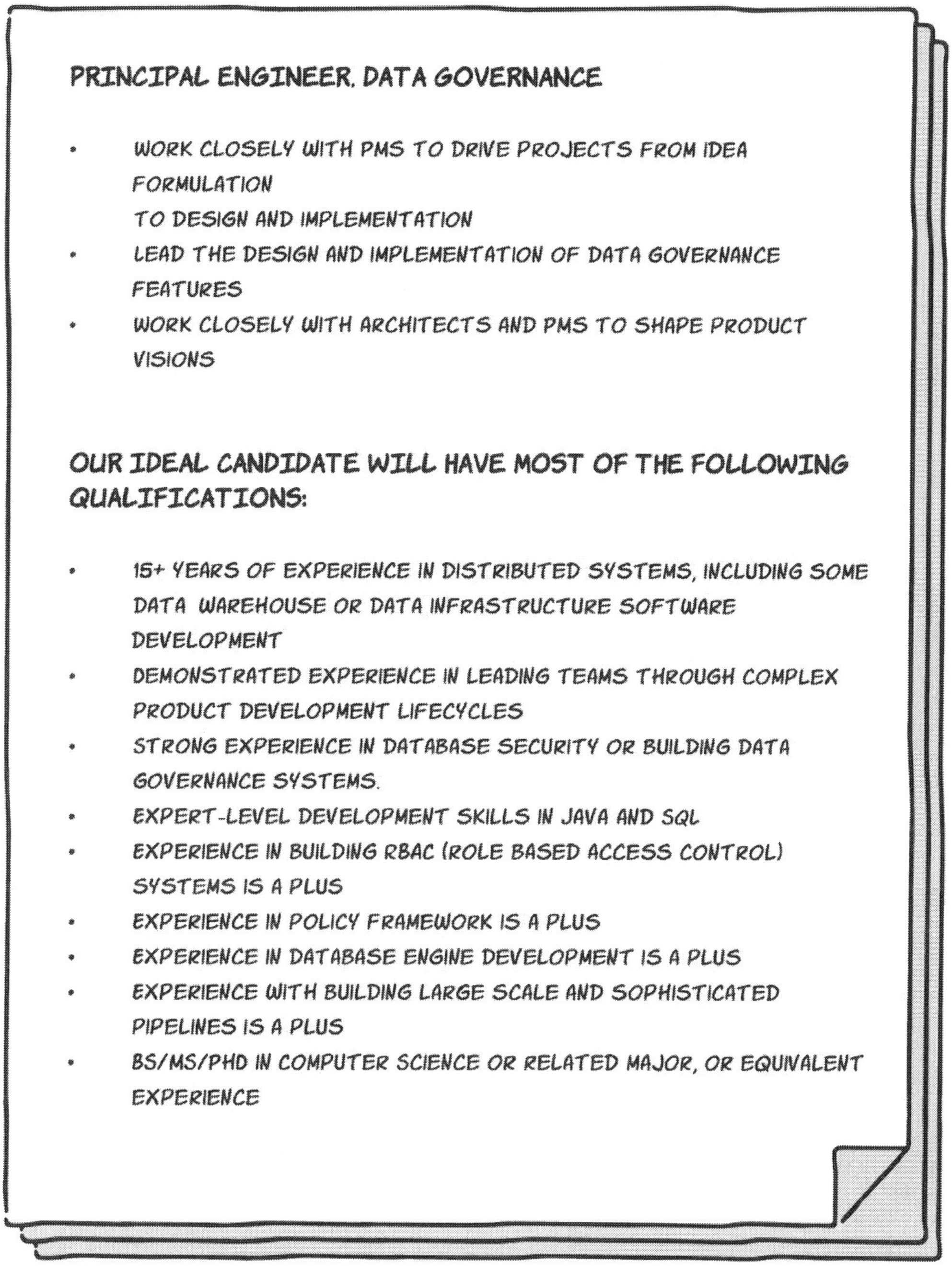

PRINCIPAL ENGINEER, DATA GOVERNANCE

- WORK CLOSELY WITH PMS TO DRIVE PROJECTS FROM IDEA FORMULATION
TO DESIGN AND IMPLEMENTATION
- LEAD THE DESIGN AND IMPLEMENTATION OF DATA GOVERNANCE FEATURES
- WORK CLOSELY WITH ARCHITECTS AND PMS TO SHAPE PRODUCT VISIONS

OUR IDEAL CANDIDATE WILL HAVE MOST OF THE FOLLOWING QUALIFICATIONS:

- 15+ YEARS OF EXPERIENCE IN DISTRIBUTED SYSTEMS, INCLUDING SOME DATA WAREHOUSE OR DATA INFRASTRUCTURE SOFTWARE DEVELOPMENT
- DEMONSTRATED EXPERIENCE IN LEADING TEAMS THROUGH COMPLEX PRODUCT DEVELOPMENT LIFECYCLES
- STRONG EXPERIENCE IN DATABASE SECURITY OR BUILDING DATA GOVERNANCE SYSTEMS.
- EXPERT-LEVEL DEVELOPMENT SKILLS IN JAVA AND SQL
- EXPERIENCE IN BUILDING RBAC (ROLE BASED ACCESS CONTROL) SYSTEMS IS A PLUS
- EXPERIENCE IN POLICY FRAMEWORK IS A PLUS
- EXPERIENCE IN DATABASE ENGINE DEVELOPMENT IS A PLUS
- EXPERIENCE WITH BUILDING LARGE SCALE AND SOPHISTICATED PIPELINES IS A PLUS
- BS/MS/PHD IN COMPUTER SCIENCE OR RELATED MAJOR, OR EQUIVALENT EXPERIENCE

[Illustration 3]

How I might diagram this position:

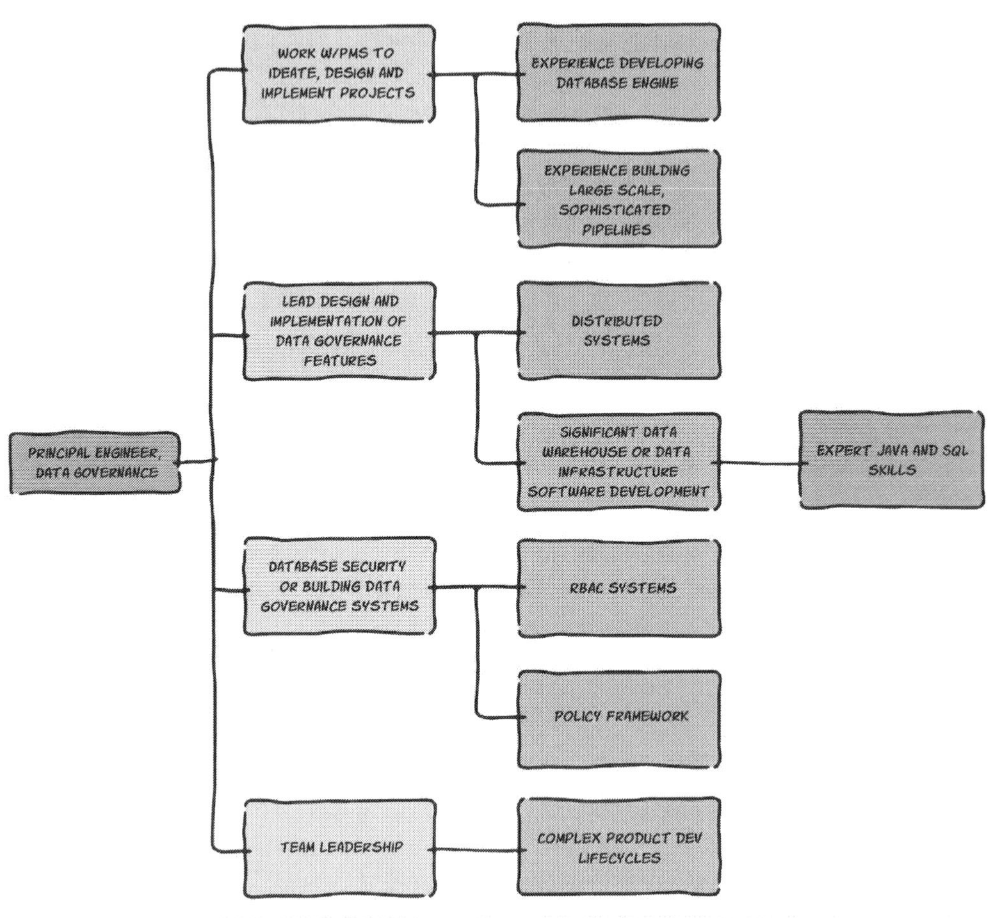

[Illustration 4]

I'll want to have some understanding of each block, and I'll want to understand what's non-negotiable, and what's nice-to-have. Starting with an organized way to think about the position was really helpful to me. It helped me (and the hiring manager) better understand what was needed, and it helped me negotiate with the manager, if I thought a particular skill set would be expensive or difficult to find. Imagine sourcing for this position without knowing what's critical, and what is a nice-to-have. Having an in-depth discussion about this early in the search will save you a ton of heartache and a ton of time later on.

It's important to start with a deeper understanding of the position and negotiate with the hiring manager. You can negotiate the addition or subtraction of a skill (what if the candidate isn't a whiz at systems design? Could you/your team teach that?) or begin to talk about the salary required to entice a fully loaded candidate. Sometimes, you might get it wrong. Always start by asking the manager if your drawing represents the role. If it doesn't, get the manager to re-draw it for you (why I always like to have a hardcopy instead of digital version of my drawing). The hiring manager might point out significant skills, or add skills, or delete some things that are not necessary. Occasionally, your drawing, which comes primarily from the job description and your understanding, is so off, you'll need to change the job posting (which was probably written in 1972!). This is a good time to work with the hiring manager to rewrite and repost it. These days I might engage ChatGPT to help me re-write it.

You might also use a breakdown like this to identify important screening questions. What's non-negotiable? To what degree should the candidate know this? What's good-better-best? Are candidates that have a "good" answer acceptable, as long as they have the ability to learn more? Or will the manager only accept candidates that know the best answer? It's important to understand -- and influence -- how the manager is thinking about the position in advance, which will help you source and screen more efficiently.

After a thorough discussion about the role with the hiring manager, you might find that your job description is outdated, inaccurate or just needs a bit of editing to appeal to top candidates. After the kickoff meeting, take a stab at writing a new description and send it to the hiring manager for final edits.

Writing a job description for publication and advertising is different than writing a job description for internal use. Yet, that is typically what I see on corporate job boards. A long, dry description of the company, bullet points of responsibilities that are often not specific enough to provide the potential candidate with a solid idea of what they will do every day and an even longer list of requirements that include everything from Microsoft Word, to "strong communication" is not helpful to you, not representative of your hiring manager or your company, and isn't helpful to the candidate.

There are plenty of resources that will help you write a better job description – my advice is that you should ensure that the posting speaks to the candidate. That said, most postings begin with a long paragraph about the company. Candidates don't read that stuff. In 2018 LinkedIn shared the results of a study of what candidates found helpful in a typical job ad. Sixty-one percent of the 450 participants cited compensation as most important, 49% said job qualifications, 49% job details, 33% said performance goals. Company culture, mission, career growth, and other details all fell below 30%. This isn't to say that information about the company isn't important to jobseekers. It just means at this beginning stage, jobseekers want to know if it's worth their time to pursue the opportunity. They want to know if there is a minimal match. As LinkedIn wrote, "[jobseekers] need to know if it's worth investing more of their time. Once they clear that hurdle, they'll have room to care about other priorities like culture, purpose and engagement."

It's also helpful at this stage to think about the market for this job. Where are the likeliest candidates? Small companies or large, in your area or should the search be broadened? Are there plenty of candidates on the market or is the candidate likely working elsewhere? A good discussion, especially when you have familiarized yourself with the market, will help the hiring manager understand how difficult or how easy it will be to find a candidate. The manager is likely to be able to provide some insight as well. If you have had the opportunity to do a bit of candidate market research and/or compensation research, share what you have learned with the manager. Explain how you have come across this information and how likely it is to be accurate. This is the kind of conversation that talent advisors and talent-focused managers love to have!

Once you have done this, you have a sourcing plan:

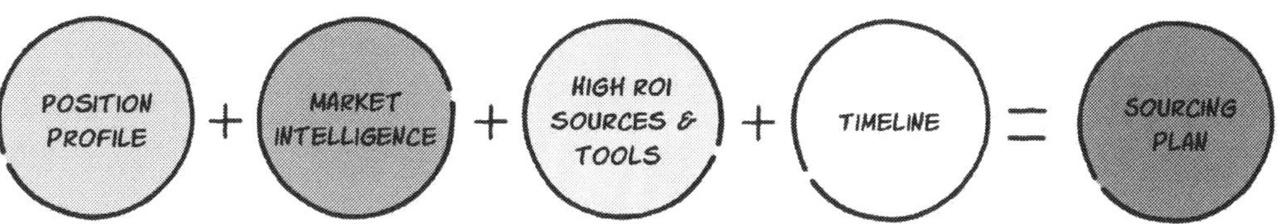

[Illustration 5]

Now, you're ready to source. But before turning your attention to the availability of external candidates, it is critical that you discuss internal candidates with your hiring manager. Let me say here, I think managers should always have at least a couple of internal candidates to interview for all but the most entry level positions. As recruiters, we can help our managers be better managers by helping them build the bench. Internal candidates bring with them all sorts of benefits, including lower cost of recruiting, decreased time spent sourcing and candidates that know the company well, have a better knowledge of how to get things done, and might require less training at the start of their tenure.

If a manager doesn't have a bench, encourage them to start building one. Encourage them to network with other managers, to hold open meetings, to meet with internal candidates who may not yet be ready for an open position but who have interest in their department. Another issue that arises is the manager's understanding of what skills and traits that could be acquired on the job and what can be obtained (often quite quickly) through job shadowing, informal or formal training or though observation. As you help a manager think about how to interview candidates, you can help them better assess internal candidates by having them think through what a new employee might learn on the job, and what must they already know on day one. Often managers forget just how little they knew when they started, and how quickly someone who is a fast learner can pick up even the most difficult responsibilities of the role.

Having an internal bench not only speeds up the process, but it can also boost hiring diverse candidates if, like most companies, your organization is more diverse at the bottom. Having this conversation with your hiring manager puts you squarely in the center of talent advising. It will be important for you, the recruiter, to ensure that your manager does not over-rely on internal candidates as well. You'll want to make sure that you introduce external candidates to the process if you see there is a pattern of relying on internal talent at the expense of including high performing, diverse talent to the mix. Remember, while you may be aware of the external market, your manager is likely not to be familiar with the limitations or possibilities of external candidates.

One last thing about the internal candidate pool. Ensure that the hiring process makes sense, and that internal candidates are screened as thoroughly (though perhaps differently) as external candidates. I have often seen managers who skip this part and later express regret, when the candidate lacks a critical skill or behavior. Require that internal candidates interview for positions and ensure that the interview team assesses the candidate against the skills and qualities that you and the manager set in advance. If you meet an internal candidate that doesn't quite meet your requirements, take the time to follow up with the candidate, provide detailed feedback on what needs to be done to get over the hump the next time.

After you have a greater understanding of the role, after you (and the hiring manager) have written the perfect job description, after you have discussed potential internal candidates, it's time to start hitting up external sources for candidates. You'll want to approach this strategically as well.

The fact is, for all but the most difficult roles, it's likely your candidates will come from a small mix of candidate sources. You will want to check your ATS to confirm your thoughts about where you're likely to find good candidates. For many roles, or at different times, merely posting the job, reviewing new candidates (and perhaps searching through the ATS for existing candidates for a recently conducted, similar search) will yield exactly what you need. Sometimes you will find that perhaps adding a source or two, like an ad on a functional job board will get you what you need.

Don't forget to have a discussion with the manager about how difficult or easy it will be to source the candidates you require. If you know that you will likely have to reach out to candidates currently solidly, happily employed, talk about the timeline required to do this well. Often managers will ask about your existing "pipeline" of candidates. Do your best to explain the myth of the candidate pipeline. There is no such thing as an instant, pre-selected list of candidates ready to jump on an opportunity for senior roles. Our recruiting orgs aren't organized in a way to organize lists of candidates "in the case" an opening becomes available. Do remind the manager that you are happy to develop any candidates or potential candidates that they have gleaned from their own networks. In fact, I expect experienced managers to always have one or two potential candidates I can reach out to at any time. And remind the managers to remind their teams of this. That's the kind of sourcing help I love!

I am a big believer in referrals (duh!) and believe that the recruiter should at least reach out to the existing employees in similar roles to obtain referrals. Recruiting is not top of mind for everyone so a weekly? (bi-weekly? monthly?) reminder to team members to submit referrals is always helpful (I'll talk more about referral programs in later in the manager section). Referrals often account for a third of hires, even though they represent a fraction of resume submittals. And, referral candidates often turn into long-term employees, when compared to candidates from other sources.

Though I can guess that it's not widely necessary, allow me to emphasize how important it is to follow up with every referred candidate, and make every attempt to share referred candidates throughout the organization. I'll talk a bit more about this in the Leadership section, but I cannot emphasize enough the importance of referrals. Even if the referred candidate is not appropriate for your open position make sure they know just how valued they are.

Third party agencies are a fact of life and can often be lifesavers. They can, however, be wedged into a manager's mind as an option preferable to the assigned corporate recruiter. There are many reasons for this – perhaps they have encountered a slow, unproductive recruiter in the past, or perhaps they have had success with a particular agency and don't want to break their luck. It's up to you – the corporate recruiter – to clearly explain the role of the corporate recruiter, the third-party recruiter, the retained search recruiter, the fees involved and the likelihood that you or the outside recruiter will be successful in the search in a timely manner. Managers may or may not be aware of the difference between contingent search and retained search. They may believe that a contingent search firm has access to different candidate pools (often, they do not) or expect that if you have engaged a retained search firm, they can remain hands off (they cannot). If you're lucky, your organization will have ironed out the rules around when a third-party recruiter can be used, and when the expense is prohibited. But I have worked in plenty of corporate environments where this wasn't clearly defined, and each manager had their own viewpoint on the subject.

When I worked in environments where it was every manager for him- or herself, I learned to talk about agency engagement up front, and get agreement from the manager about how and when we'd get an agency involved. Most of the time, I was tasked by HR leadership with alleviating the use of third-party agencies, especially where there were recruiters who could do just as good a job. This was not always easy. When I meet with a manager who likes to rely on the third-party agencies or search firms, I first try to understand why. Could it be the knowledge of the market and viable candidates? Can't blame a manager for wanting to have in-depth conversations about talent, talent competitors and market knowledge. If you, as the corporate recruiter, cannot have discussions at this level, then it's time to up your game or bring in someone from the recruiting team that can participate in these kinds of discussions! Or, could it be that the external recruiter provides a higher level of service, responding quickly, providing data, clearing paths? Again, that means that the corporate recruiter must up the game!

If you decide (or have no choice) to work with an agency, I propose that you set up an agency kickoff at the start of every search. This is your opportunity to ensure that the agency earns the fee by making you more productive and more successful from the start. Make sure that you, the agency and the hiring manager are aligned on the sourcing strategy. And, for something as important as sourcing strategy, you must be there. Do not allow the agency recruiter to meet with the manager without you. If you aren't present, it's likely that you will miss out on important information that not only informs sourcing, but will likely inform selection as well, and you need to know this information.

I'd like to underscore here, if you haven't picked up on it already, that you – the corporate recruiter -- remain highly engaged with the agency throughout the process and that you retain control of how decisions get made and the timeliness of completing the work. That's how you add value to the process.

Set up a regular check-in meeting with the agency recruiter and share how you expect the process, including the interview process, will proceed. Make sure the agency knows exactly how to submit candidates (many ATS systems allow direct submission) and whether you will review candidates before submitting to the manager or if they should submit candidates directly to the manager. Often, good agencies will submit a summary of their interview with the candidates and here, you should take note. The interview notes submitted by agencies are often highly valued by hiring managers. You would do well to take note and to discuss with your manager what they find valuable about the external recruiter notes, and present candidates that you source in the same way. Takes more time, for sure, but often your candidates are being rejected by hiring managers because they don't understand why you're presenting the candidate. Or perhaps they don't believe that you're capable of screening candidates thoroughly. A brief, well-structured way of presenting candidates provides an easy, apparent way of discussing all candidates and shows the hiring manager the value that comes with screening the candidates. Pro tip: create a standard version of a candidate submittal [example in appendix] and share with the agency, so that every candidate submitted is shared in the same way, with the same information summarized.

It's also important to spend a bit of time up front with the agency, agreeing on how, and how often, you will keep the agency updated, how they will report on their progress, agree on a timeline, and make sure the agency recruiter is well versed on the skills and qualities required. We'll talk more about the interview strategy in the next chapters, but it is critical at the screening stage to understand and screen for the required skills and traits, and to commit to screening candidates for the minimum level of skills and traits needed to do the job.

The next sourcing topic is foundational – your ATS and any job board postings that yield relevant candidates. Let's start with your ATS, which is where you will gather new applicants, where you find candidates who have applied, as well as house candidates that you found through direct sourcing or other methods. And lastly – perhaps most importantly – it's where you will find candidates that were applicable for other similar roles. While these candidates may be passive (i.e., not looking for a new position) they may very well be appropriate for your current job, and with a little nudging, might become interested in your current role. Depends on your needs.

Some jobs require a minimal sourcing plan. Check for internal candidates, referrals, and applicants. If that's how you know you will find candidates, then I recommend that you don't spend time sourcing from other pools, unless you aren't seeing diversity from these sources.

If, however, you need to widen your search, then I recommend first posting to job boards and secondly, searching your ATS for candidates attached to closed positions. The second group of candidates is perhaps more passive than the first, but it's likely they are still interested in your company and, if the timing is right, would consider a similar position. If you get into the habit of checking candidates that already exist in your ATS, you may be able to save yourself time, engage with candidates that already want to engage with your company and you may be able to source candidates quickly.

If you need to widen your search and cast a wider net for active candidates, you'll want to post to job boards. Before meeting with your manager, do a bit homework. Explore what's worked in the past, find out if there are any industry or functional boards that work well. If you're not well-versed in sourcing for this type of position, or want to increase your sourcing knowledge, I recommend experimenting with one or two sites to see how they perform for you. Here is a list of job board types that I collected from ChatGPT, and of course you can find many specific recommendations on RecruiterHunt.com.

1. General job boards: These job boards feature a wide variety of job listings across different industries and job functions. Examples include LinkedIn, Indeed, Monster and Glassdoor.

2. Niche job boards: These job boards focus on specific industries or job functions, such as healthcare, technology, or finance. Examples include Health eCareers, Dice and eFinancialCareers.

3. Freelance job boards: These job boards feature project-based or freelance job opportunities for independent contractors. Examples include Upwork and Freelancer.

4. Geographic job boards: These job boards focus on job listings within a specific geographic region, such as a city, state, or country. Examples include ZipRecruiter, Jobing and Workopolis.

5. Diversity and inclusion job boards: These job boards focus on job opportunities for underrepresented groups, such as women, people of color, LGBTQ individuals, and individuals with disabilities. Examples include DiversityJobs, Hirepurpose and Out & Equal.

6. Government job boards: These job boards feature job opportunities with government agencies, including federal, state and local governments. Examples include USAJobs and GovtJobs.

7. Education job boards: These job boards focus on job opportunities in education, including K-12 schools, colleges and universities. Examples include HigherEdJobs and SchoolSpring.

8. Executive job boards: These job boards feature job opportunities for senior-level executives, including CEOs, CFOs, and other C-suite positions. Examples include ExecuNet and BlueSteps.

9. Remote job boards: These job boards feature job opportunities that can be done remotely from anywhere in the world. Examples include Remote.co and We Work Remotely.

Referrals are perhaps my favorite method of collecting external candidates for positions, primarily because referrals tend to stay longer, and because they are generally able to navigate the organization better and faster. I will discuss setting up referral programs in the leadership portion of the book, but I want to ensure that you're leveraging the entire company to help you find great candidates for your open positions.

First things first. Ensure that your hiring manager, and the interviewers (and anyone else on the team) understand the importance of referrals (in most companies, referrals represent a third of all hires). Some managers/team members may harbor the idea that collecting referrals is your job as the recruiter. Explain (patiently, please) that your job is to find candidates that might not be familiar with anyone at the company, and you're doing that, through posting and direct sourcing (you should explain this – managers don't know that we do it) but we know that often people know great people who work for other organizations who may not be aware of our opportunities. Explain the advantage of tapping into candidate pools where the talent is known, the advantage of being able to pursue a candidate who is not known by your talent competitors and the advantage that the referrer offers the candidate – the assurance that moving to a new environment is a good decision.

Additionally, we know that we can move quickly with referred candidates (and they are known to make decisions to join more quickly). That said, managers and hiring teams may still be unsure of how to refer a candidate, or they may be uncertain about who qualifies as a referral. It's our job as the recruiter to ensure that they understand the program.

When I was at Yahoo, I had the chance to build out the employee referral program and experiment with methods and tools. It was an unusual situation – the CEO of the company wanted to send a message to competitors – and I had free reign (and a pretty big budget) to increase tech candidates by any means possible. I'll share more in the leadership section, but I'm here to tell you that some of the simplest solutions had the biggest impact. For example, prior to launch, we looked at the referral data, and saw that referrals had dwindled to single digits every day, from hundreds of referrals submitted every day. We decided to survey a small sample of employees. What we learned was that, at that time, Yahoos were unsure about how to answer questions from their peers about what was happening at the company. We provided a pretty simple tent card with an FAQ that answered the most common questions and placed them on the lunch tables and posted the info on the company intranet. It worked! Just giving employees the words to use helped them understand and communicate the environment to their referrals. We did many other things, but first we had to make sure that employees felt comfortable referring their friends. Since then, I have included a referral FAQ in my best practices bag. Before any referral effort – large or small – make sure that you explain the benefits of referrals, why referred candidates are needed, and why referral candidates might find this a better environment than your talent competitors. It's important to do this online (or even hardcopy tent cards!) as well as during your discussions with hiring managers, interviewers and even the team at large.

It's worthwhile to consider other showman-like tactics to gather referrals – referral lunches, contests, prizes for specific types of referrals, etc. All of these can be effective ways of getting the candidates you need. And of course, you can encourage team members to solicit referrals via their networks by making it easy to share open positions on social networks or via LinkedIn. I highly recommend that you send a reminder to team members when opening an important req, or at least quarterly. For a very targeted effort, gather team members in a room for a referral party (back in the day, I would provide beer and snacks as inducements), where you share pre-written emails and LinkedIn announcements so that team members can share with their networks. Often, people don't feel comfortable reaching out to people they don't know, so getting them to point out people they have worked with, or know about, with good reputations, and having the employee simply pass that name along to you, the recruiter, is all that's needed. You can take it from there!

A word about referrals. Employees refer their friends for a number of reasons. Mainly because they like to be helpful to their friends and employers, and because they want to work with people who have proven they can be successful. As I learned at Yahoo, employees will not refer their friends if they are unsure about the environment, or if they're not certain their friends will be treated well. Given that referrals have such a high likelihood of being hired, it's important that we treat all referrals well. At Yahoo, our referral program got a ton of recognition from leadership and the C-suite. Sure, we were able to deliver hires, but I firmly believe that we were awarded a big company prize because we were extra attentive to every referral we received. We ensured that follow-up was timely and personalized where possible. And we followed up not only with the candidate, but with the referring employee as well. And where the messaging had to be automated, we updated the language in the ATS to be as accurate as possible. Our efforts did not go unnoticed!

Let's turn our attention to direct sourcing – the art of finding and engaging candidates who are unaware of your open position, who haven't applied or haven't been referred. It's often the first thought when sourcing is mentioned. Though it is necessary, in some cases, to find the right candidates through direct sourcing, it is the toughest way to generate them.

I talked about diagramming positions earlier in this chapter. This is when a specific, verified-by-the-hiring-manager diagram becomes especially helpful. Direct sourcing, at least the finding suitable candidates part, done well, should not take a lot of time. If you're clear about the skills for which you are hiring, and you and the hiring manager have identified some distinguishing factors (such as tough-to-find skills, suitable companies from which you'd like to poach some good folks, etc.), you should be able to unearth a handful of passive candidates and start making calls. It might even be helpful to work with your manager to identify people and start making calls. If your offer is matched well (your company/job offers more than what their current company offers) you may have good luck in your first round of calls and outreach. If the people you approach are happy in their current role, then make a new friend, note that they're not interested at this time, and ask for a referral. It's been my experience that getting referrals is the most important part of a direct sourcing campaign.

Keep in mind that direct sourcing can be risky business. While you're able to target the exact candidates needed, you're presented with a big challenge when it comes to closing them. If you reach out to someone who is happy at their job, entice them with something new, you still are working from a deficit. The candidate may agree to kick the tires at your organization, but you might find it difficult to entice them to accept a job offer.

I won't go deep into campus recruiting in this book, except to say that it is important to develop campus relationships – to the extent that you're able to massage them into being a good source of candidates. Think about campus hiring as a strong underpinning of your overall talent strategy. That is, look into future, think about what you might need, and leverage campus hires to fill the need. For example, if you know that digital marketing is a strength your company needs to develop, look at bringing in campus interns and hires to fill the need from easily accessible college programs that graduate students with those skills. Also keep in mind that college hiring can be a strong source of diverse candidates.

If you are starting a college program, work with a hiring manager and their team to select a couple of campus programs and leverage the team to develop deep relationships with professors and administration to make sure your company is known, and great students are referred to you. If your company has a well-established campus recruiting program, make sure that your org is connected to key administrators, instructors and professors, that you are involved with selection and setting criteria, and that your hiring managers and interviewers are involved. Make sure your hiring managers understand the importance of setting aside a few reqs to ensure there is place for interns and college hires to land. Everyone loves college recruiting when they're asked to return to their alma mater and turn on the charm. Those same managers, however, hide in the shadows when it comes time to give up a req for a college hire. Figure out a way to help managers bridge the gap. Perhaps the headcount ask doesn't kick in for a year. Highlight the success of campus recruiting efforts at every opportunity; you may need to highlight this success in the case of budget cutbacks.

Lastly, I recommend extensive training before sending employees to campus to interview students. Send only your best interviewers, those who know how to assess for skills and characteristics. Spend some time determining what characteristics are most important to succeed in your organization, and spend time assessing for these qualities, as you will have little else to assess. Most college students, you will find, have generally the same level of knowledge or skill.

What sets them apart are soft skills – how hard will they work on new problems, or learning about something new, how they communicate, and how their communication style matches the expectations of your organization. These are the kind of traits that will help you differentiate students and figure out who will work best in your environment.

Of course, sourcing doesn't end when you find top candidates on a job board or get a ton of referrals. In fact, I would say the job of sourcing is just getting started at this stage. Your next steps are to reach out to the candidates, get them engaged and interested, figure out if they are indeed a great match, connect them to the hiring manager or next qualifier, then set them up for what comes next or decline them. That's five steps, and at any point things could fall apart, leaving a hole in your search. That's why we're *talent advisors* – because we know that recruiting is a process filled with unforeseen surprises, for which we're unflappably prepared!

Reaching out to Candidates

You may find the candidate in your ATS, or the candidate might be direct sourced with only a dubious email address available. Doesn't matter. You've got to get the candidate's attention. With candidates who apply, this shouldn't be too difficult. An email introduction is fine, and you can ask the candidate to set up a time for an initial discussion using an online calendar app, such as Calendly (check out recruiterhunt.com for additional tools) or perhaps your ATS offers this feature. Make sure that your intro email contains all the relevant information about this meeting and suggests ways for the candidate to learn about your organization.

For candidates that you have sourced online, where you may not be certain that you have the correct email address, or perhaps you're starting from scratch, I recommend spending 5 minutes max searching for the proper address or phone number. To find contact info, try these tactics (https://www.lusha.com/blog/how-to-find-someones-email-address-by-name/) or these (https://ahrefs.com/blog/find-email-address/).

Because we all spend so much time online, and often use different communication strategies with each of our online presences, I recommend that you send the outreach email to as many email addresses available to you, except the work email address. If you have access to their email address at their current employer, proceed with caution. Only use this address if you have no other, or if you aren't getting a response. I have sourcing friends that would never reach out to a candidate's work contact info, but I say if you can't get to the candidate any other way, proceed, but cautiously. And always offer to switch to a preferred communication method if the candidate wishes.

And don't forget the phone. Not so long ago, it was the first step in candidate outreach. Times change, people use their phones for voice messaging far less than they used to. After leaving a voicemail, I suggest leaving a brief text message to let the candidate know that you are quite interested in speaking with them.

That said, I recommend a 1-2-3-4 punch when it comes to candidate outreach. At the same time, I send an email, a LinkedIn Inmail and I leave a phone message, backed up by a brief text message. In the phone message I introduce myself briefly and let them know that I'm reaching out about a position (or because I want to chat about their career) and I let them know that I've left more details in email and LinkedIn. With this approach, you let the candidate know that you're serious about reaching them, that you're willing to meet them wherever they are most comfortable.

Writing effective email is a subject that will continuously command your attention. I know some recruiters who constantly experiment with new approaches or adapt their approach, depending on the position for which they are recruiting. Some vary after reading the candidate's profile. I've always been a fan of the straight-ahead approach. Give them just enough info to draw them in and want more. And give them enough info to let them know that you deeply understand the position and you are reaching out to them, specifically. I don't recommend sharing the job description at this early stage. The idea is that you're interested in learning about them, where they are in their career, how happy they are at their current company. Leave the position matchmaking to the second interaction. Your first goal is to get to know them, and for them to learn a bit about you and the company. You could skip this, but I warn you, that without this kind of foundation, you may find yourself in for a surprise at a critical point down the line.

I've shared my favorite outreach example in the appendix, and following is an OK example from ChatGPT:

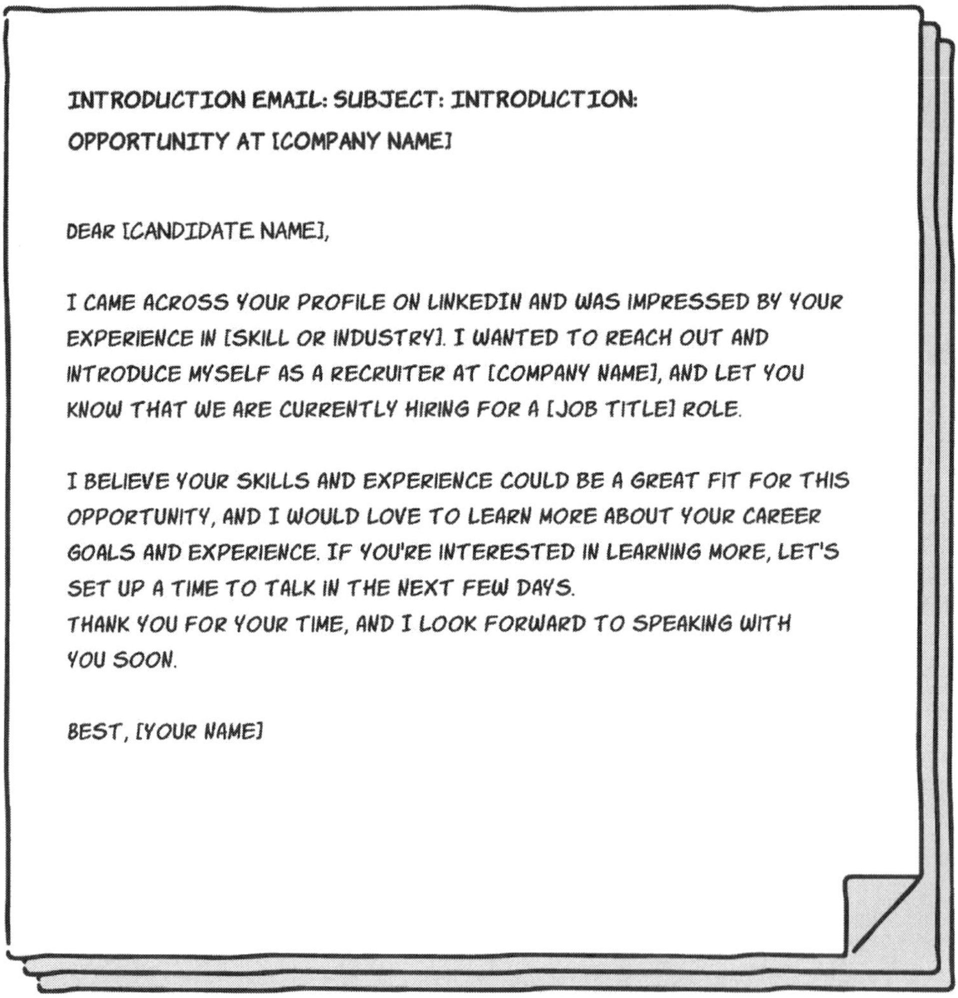

INTRODUCTION EMAIL: SUBJECT: INTRODUCTION: OPPORTUNITY AT [COMPANY NAME]

DEAR [CANDIDATE NAME],

I CAME ACROSS YOUR PROFILE ON LINKEDIN AND WAS IMPRESSED BY YOUR EXPERIENCE IN [SKILL OR INDUSTRY]. I WANTED TO REACH OUT AND INTRODUCE MYSELF AS A RECRUITER AT [COMPANY NAME], AND LET YOU KNOW THAT WE ARE CURRENTLY HIRING FOR A [JOB TITLE] ROLE.

I BELIEVE YOUR SKILLS AND EXPERIENCE COULD BE A GREAT FIT FOR THIS OPPORTUNITY, AND I WOULD LOVE TO LEARN MORE ABOUT YOUR CAREER GOALS AND EXPERIENCE. IF YOU'RE INTERESTED IN LEARNING MORE, LET'S SET UP A TIME TO TALK IN THE NEXT FEW DAYS.
THANK YOU FOR YOUR TIME, AND I LOOK FORWARD TO SPEAKING WITH YOU SOON.

BEST, [YOUR NAME]

[Illustration 7]

This is OK, but my recommendation is that your first email should contain a bit of personal information so that the candidate knows that you're reaching out to them, specifically. When you personalize your approach, you're likely to have greater, quicker follow-up.

You'll want to test your email language, to see what works. I believe that shorter, personalized messages work best, but you might find that your candidates, your field, or your location prefers differently. Keep track of your results and save your email language for future use.

Lastly, I was recently reminded of a tactic we employed during the early days of my sourcing career. At the high-end, retained search agency where I first learned this business, we regularly sourced candidates' phone and home addresses. We'd find a reasonable number of candidates for a high-end search and send a very nice package of material, including the job description and a personalized letter. We'd also leave a message for the candidate on the day the package arrived. This is a bit more time-consuming, and a bit more expensive, but it worked with a high percentage of prospects. Definitely worth the time and dollars if you are having difficulty reaching a candidate online, via email or phone.

TL;DR

- Figure out what you're looking for, both in terms of skills and candidate quality. Go deep. Outline the position, if that helps, and ensure your hiring manager is aligned with your understanding. Return to this understanding to ensure interviewers understand the position.

- Understand the talent market for the position and negotiate the right amount of time needed to do the job. Share your sourcing plan with your hiring manager. Look for internal candidates first, and encourage hiring managers to build a bench.

- Working with agencies is sometimes necessary. Make sure that you work alongside them, helping them to be successful. Over time, eliminate the use of agencies that aren't necessary. Pay attention to the way external agencies present candidates, and ensure that all candidates are presented the same way.

- Continuously test and adjust your outreach to candidates.

Chapter 5 - Screening Candidates

Once you have found candidates you think might be appropriate for the position, it's time to screen them. While you're not the hiring manager, your job is to determine if this prospect, heretofore only known for what's on their resume, has the potential to succeed in the role. This is where you move from paper pusher to recruiter. You are placing bets on candidates. You'd better be certain that your bets are aligned with your hiring manager's. Your job here is to learn a bit more about the candidate's experience, their interest in a new role, their salary requirements, and to make the initial determination that the candidate is indeed appropriate for the role.

Prior to screening, work with the hiring manager to determine how you will decide which candidates make the cut. In your kickoff meeting, or in a subsequent meeting about sourcing, you have outlined the most important responsibilities of the job. Identify the most important skills, and talk with the manager about expectations, and how they might screen for this skill. Test the boundaries – at what point would they consider a candidate at this level acceptable, and what is an example of hitting the ball out of the park? This kind of information will help you as you're screening candidates and deciding whether or not to send them to the interview stage. A recruiter, a talent advisor, has an opinion and makes a judgement. A baby recruiter simply passes along the information. Occasionally, you will have difficulty determining if a prospect would make a good candidate. At this stage, it's OK to send along to the manager, noting your concern and learning from the manager, so that the next time, you're better able to determine if the candidate fits the position. Don't do this too much though, and don't forget to learn from passing along a candidate. In fact, until you're super confident, keep a record of your screens:accepts. By monitoring this ratio, you will be able to improve your sourcing, by asking candidates better, more targeted questions. My goal was to always get to 100% alignment with the hiring manager – to get to the place where every candidate I submitted was accepted by the hiring manager. In a few instances, I became so aligned with the hiring manager that the hiring manager determined that they didn't need to conduct screens. Most of the time I hovered somewhere around 50-60% of my candidates being accepted. If it isn't obvious, I'm a bit competitive, so I enjoyed trying to beat my own record.

Submitting screened candidates to the hiring manager is an important part of the process. This is where you can provide a bit of persuasion and highlight the candidate's assets and point to areas that you recommend the hiring manager spend more time. This, I believe, is how we earn our donuts. We help managers and interviewers focus more deeply on their areas of expertise by first tackling some of the easier parts of understanding a candidate's background.

How you submit screened candidates for review is important. It is often the difference between manager's preference for agency candidates over your candidates. A brief note, with vitals, and a few words about why you think this candidate might be successful, and a few words about areas to probe is helpful to the manager. It is also helpful to you. This kind of summary makes you think a bit more deeply about the kind of candidate who will be successful, and helps you improve your hit rate. Being able to quickly assess a candidate's ability to be successful leads to faster, more successful sourcing, as well as underscores the alignment you have with the hiring manager. I knew that I was getting better at identifying great candidates when managers asked me to schedule candidates for interviews without the manager screen! Below is a sample of an email to send with each screened candidate. Remember to make your subject line consistent so that managers or screeners can easily find your email.

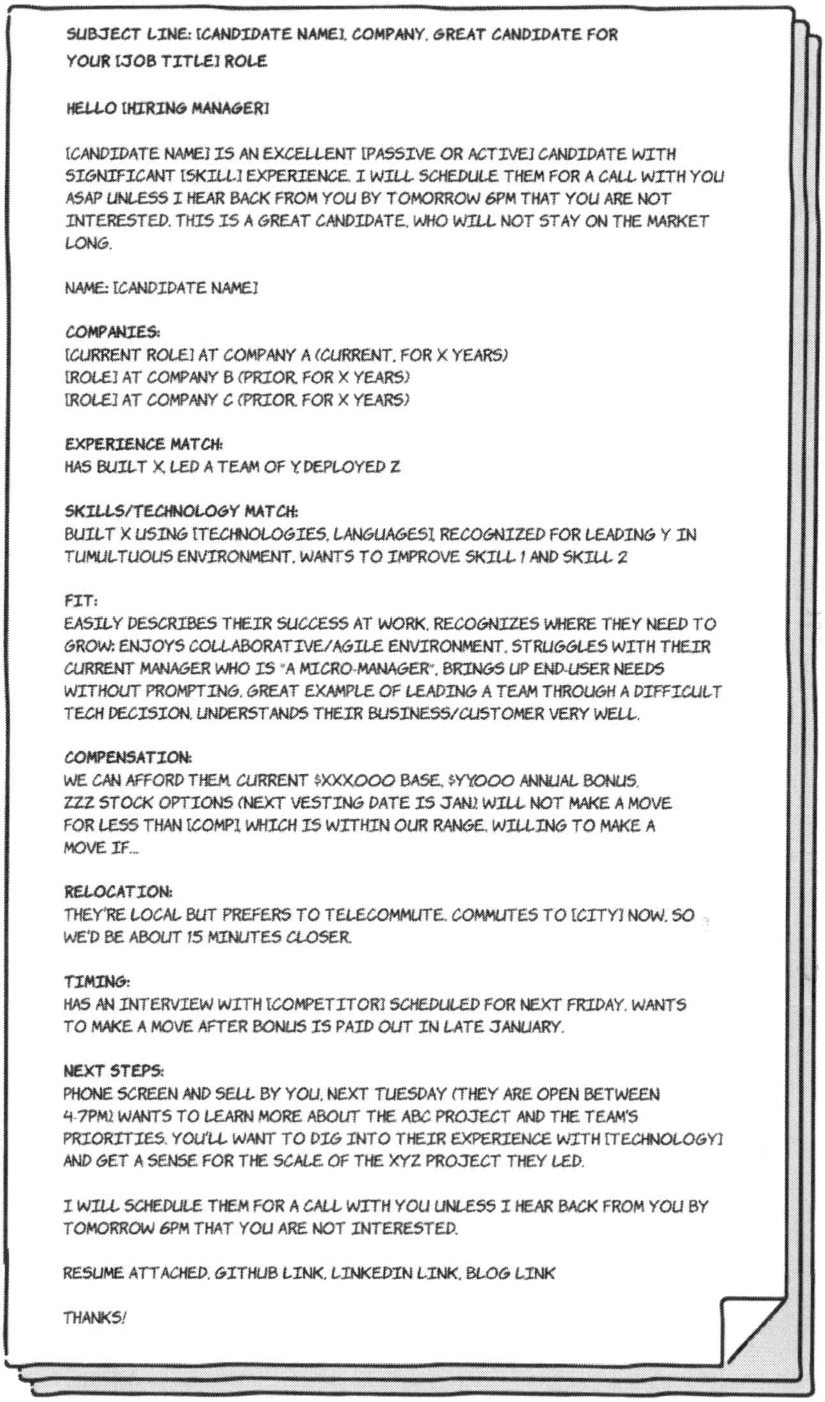

SUBJECT LINE: [CANDIDATE NAME], COMPANY, GREAT CANDIDATE FOR YOUR [JOB TITLE] ROLE

HELLO [HIRING MANAGER]

[CANDIDATE NAME] IS AN EXCELLENT [PASSIVE OR ACTIVE] CANDIDATE WITH SIGNIFICANT [SKILL] EXPERIENCE. I WILL SCHEDULE THEM FOR A CALL WITH YOU ASAP UNLESS I HEAR BACK FROM YOU BY TOMORROW 6PM THAT YOU ARE NOT INTERESTED. THIS IS A GREAT CANDIDATE, WHO WILL NOT STAY ON THE MARKET LONG.

NAME: [CANDIDATE NAME]

COMPANIES:
[CURRENT ROLE] AT COMPANY A (CURRENT, FOR X YEARS)
[ROLE] AT COMPANY B (PRIOR, FOR X YEARS)
[ROLE] AT COMPANY C (PRIOR, FOR X YEARS)

EXPERIENCE MATCH:
HAS BUILT X, LED A TEAM OF Y, DEPLOYED Z

SKILLS/TECHNOLOGY MATCH:
BUILT X USING [TECHNOLOGIES, LANGUAGES], RECOGNIZED FOR LEADING Y IN TUMULTUOUS ENVIRONMENT, WANTS TO IMPROVE SKILL 1 AND SKILL 2

FIT:
EASILY DESCRIBES THEIR SUCCESS AT WORK, RECOGNIZES WHERE THEY NEED TO GROW; ENJOYS COLLABORATIVE/AGILE ENVIRONMENT, STRUGGLES WITH THEIR CURRENT MANAGER WHO IS "A MICRO-MANAGER", BRINGS UP END-USER NEEDS WITHOUT PROMPTING, GREAT EXAMPLE OF LEADING A TEAM THROUGH A DIFFICULT TECH DECISION, UNDERSTANDS THEIR BUSINESS/CUSTOMER VERY WELL.

COMPENSATION:
WE CAN AFFORD THEM. CURRENT $XXX,000 BASE, $YY,000 ANNUAL BONUS, ZZZ STOCK OPTIONS (NEXT VESTING DATE IS JAN). WILL NOT MAKE A MOVE FOR LESS THAN [COMP], WHICH IS WITHIN OUR RANGE. WILLING TO MAKE A MOVE IF...

RELOCATION:
THEY'RE LOCAL BUT PREFERS TO TELECOMMUTE. COMMUTES TO [CITY] NOW, SO WE'D BE ABOUT 15 MINUTES CLOSER.

TIMING:
HAS AN INTERVIEW WITH [COMPETITOR] SCHEDULED FOR NEXT FRIDAY. WANTS TO MAKE A MOVE AFTER BONUS IS PAID OUT IN LATE JANUARY.

NEXT STEPS:
PHONE SCREEN AND SELL BY YOU, NEXT TUESDAY (THEY ARE OPEN BETWEEN 4-7PM). WANTS TO LEARN MORE ABOUT THE ABC PROJECT AND THE TEAM'S PRIORITIES. YOU'LL WANT TO DIG INTO THEIR EXPERIENCE WITH [TECHNOLOGY] AND GET A SENSE FOR THE SCALE OF THE XYZ PROJECT THEY LED.

I WILL SCHEDULE THEM FOR A CALL WITH YOU UNLESS I HEAR BACK FROM YOU BY TOMORROW 6PM THAT YOU ARE NOT INTERESTED.

RESUME ATTACHED, GITHUB LINK, LINKEDIN LINK, BLOG LINK

THANKS!

[Illustration 8]

It's important to keep track of your sourcing efforts/success. Track sourcing in your ATS, of course. Or you may have access to a CRM, where you capture potential leads and track the progress of outreach efforts. I also kept a spreadsheet of candidates I thought I might reach out to again. I kept a list like this for years. At least once or twice a year I would send a friendly email newsletter to these candidates, with some updates on what was happening in the TA world (salary surveys, best employer links, stories about my organization, etc.). I'm sure many deleted the emails without so much as reading them. But a few stayed in touch, would always take my call, occasionally referred great candidates and appreciated being part of my network.

It's also important to learn from mistakes when sourcing. Nobody likes to re-start the engine every time. So take a moment to carefully close out a search once you have submitted a slate of likely candidates to your hiring manager. Make sure you have captured all contact info, and that you updated their profiles in your ATS, CRM or personal list. Additionally, create a place in your database to capture your sourcing methods. Best sources, search strings that performed for you, any notes that will be helpful should you or a colleague should have to launch a similar search in the future.

I know many recruiters who despise this part of the process – you have to kiss a lot of frogs. But if your desire is to become valued by your business and less replaceable by an AI tool, then you will understand the importance of only presenting well-vetted candidates to your hiring managers.

During the kickoff process you will have at least started the conversation about skills and characteristics of the successful candidate. During the sourcing process, it's likely that you learned a lot more about the candidate profile. Take a few minutes to review what you have learned and create at least three questions that will help you separate acceptable, OK candidates, from superstars. This is important. I often find that recruiters do not use their valuable time to really distinguish between a candidate that meets the criteria and one who will blow away manager's expectations.

It's harder to do this for some roles, like technical positions, but still worth the try. Over time you will find that your ability to screen in and screen out acceptable candidates will expand. Especially if you recruit for the same team each time. Again, I found it helpful to measure just how successful my screening efforts were – always aiming for 100% of my submittals to be accepted by the hiring team. Usually, after working with a hiring manager and team, after two or three reqs, I could get a pretty good hit rate.

Screening, as fun as it may be, can't go on forever. Make sure you have put in place an understanding of timelines and the number of candidates you will present. Revisit your conversation about timelines and completion date at the strategy meeting, and at every follow-up meeting, as you begin submitting screened candidates to managers, and confirm that they are still on board (renegotiate the dates if meetings or vacations or work may delay the process). After you have submitted the agreed upon number of candidates, be sure to meet with your managers to discuss each candidate, what the manager liked (or didn't like) about each candidate, what more needs be explored or learned about each candidate, who will move forward in the process and next steps.

What you should learn during a candidate screen

1. A good understanding of their current role. What they are responsible for, the kind of team they're on (or lead), major projects they have worked on or completed. Your job here is to find out what the candidate excels at, what they like to do, what they're interested in next. It's also important to get a sense of their limits, what they would like to learn next and what new skills, methods or technologies excite them.

2. Take a few minutes to thoroughly describe the job responsibilities. Have they had this experience? Examples? What would they like to learn?

3. Desired salary, relocation needs, travel, current exact title, approximate availability date.

4. Don't forget to provide the candidate with a realistic job preview (number of team members, current focus, etc.)

5. Don't forget to emphasize some of the great things this job offers the candidate (access to a wonderful manager, an engaged team, more prestige, a promotion, etc.)

Becoming a fast, accurate screener is how you earn your stripes as a recruiter. It's not something I learned to do overnight. It took me some years to become an excellent identifier of talent. So much went into this; understanding the role in-depth, understanding the hiring manager's preferences, my willingness to share my assessment of the candidate, consistently sharing candidate screens in a way that could be digested and compared. Once I mastered these skills, I found that my hiring managers appreciated and relied on my influence and ability to bring great candidates to the table. And I came to better understand and appreciate the value that I brought to the organization – ensuring that managers got introduced to the best talent in the market!

All that said, keep in mind that your managers – especially less experienced managers – have a voracious appetite for candidates. Remind them of the process (screen-interview-DECIDE) at every opportunity. If they reject all of your screened candidates, then you and the manager must sit down and figure out what's missing from the candidate profile, how you should change the search or what they want that doesn't exist in high quantity in the market. If it comes down to finding and screening additional candidates, discuss the impact that this will have to the timeline. And remind the manager, however gently, that you will not play the game of endless screening and interviewing. Your job is to get the manager comfortable enough to make decisions and enthusiastic enough to hire a candidate. I once sat in a meeting with one of my frustrated recruiters, who was working with a hiring manager who couldn't (or wouldn't) make a decision. I empathized that it was difficult to pull the trigger and how compelling it was to keep hoping that a better candidate would turn up. But I (as the recruiting leader) just couldn't apply unlimited resources to this req (thinly veiled threat). Was he impressed with the candidate that the hiring team had interviewed? Did he believe that the candidate could do the job and increase the team's productivity? Could we afford the candidate? Then, I advised, he should move forward. Yes, it was possible that he could find a better candidate, but at what cost? Time? More money? I even promised to help if things didn't work out well (accepting part of the responsibility is especially important to new or inexperienced managers). Needless to say, the candidate started, did a great job and I never heard a peep from the hiring manager. Sometimes a bit of confidence is all that's needed, and sometimes that confidence comes from a talent advisor!

TL;DR

- Great sourcing starts with an open conversation with your hiring manager, where you and the manager share your understanding of the important aspects of position – both skills and behaviors.

- Start sourcing by first understanding if there are internal candidates. Get your hiring managers in the habit of helping employees understand what it takes to be considered.

- Reach out via phone, text, email and LinkedIn simultaneously. Your job is to reach the candidate, then find out what type of communication is preferred. Don't stop at one outreach. Stop at 8 or 9 attempts.

- After screening candidates, take the time to submit a standardized, detailed call report. It will make a difference!

- Remind managers that their job is to screen, interview and decide. If they are having trouble making a decision, it is because they are unclear about their needs. Offer to review the profile and help them set the stage for decision-making.

Chapter 6 - Embedding Diversity in Your Recruiting Practices

A short story here. A long, long, long time ago I'd recently exited college and was thrust upon the real world. Upon using up all my savings on clubbing and fancy outfits, I figured out that I needed a job. Pronto. So I did what a lot of people – especially women – did in those days. I signed up at an employment agency. I took a typing test (in those days I was pretty fast) and impressed the temp recruiter. She had an immediate assignment for me. The next day, I was ordered to report to an architectural firm. They needed someone to answer the phones and do other clerical work. I was ecstatic! I'd had a slight interest in architecture when I was in middle school (this is another story for another day; ask me about it over drinks!), maybe this would be my introduction to a new career path!

I arrived the next morning at the beautiful downtown Chicago office, a bit early. I wanted to make a good impression. There was no one behind the reception desk, I assumed that's where I'd be assigned. I found someone and let them know that I had arrived, ready to work! She asked me to wait in the lobby until she figured out where I was to report. I waited in the lobby, blissfully imagining myself as an architect, designing skyscrapers, winning big awards, using the compass expertly, for 15 minutes or so. I went back to remind them that I was still in the lobby, ready to report to work.

I sat in the lobby for another 20 minutes. Still no direction. After waiting for 20 minutes longer the associate came out to the lobby to tell me that they would not need my services after all. I would be paid for the time contracted. I left the building, confused, and headed back to the temp agency. They assured me that I would be paid. No one looked me in the eye.

I suspected that the architectural firm didn't want a black woman at the front desk. I had no proof, no confirmation, just a feeling. I also made a promise to myself, not knowing that I would end up in recruiting. If I ever worked anywhere and had any influence, no one would sit in a lobby and leave wondering if they'd been passed over because of their race.

I shared this story because it is instructive for recruiting teams. We must communicate as much information as possible about our process, about what we expect from candidates and what they can expect from us. We must do this consistently and we must be respectful of every candidate.

Diversifying the organization often rests with the recruiting team. This isn't right, but it is often so. I won't use this soapbox to scold corporate America, but if you are only looking to recruiting to improve diversity results, it will take you a long time to get there.

So let's start at the place where it has been determined that the team needs to diversify. I believe that, to get to this point, the hiring manager (and often someone higher up in the organization) must seriously review their team and, along with the team's HR leader, determine where to best focus efforts. It's important to do this long before a position opens, so that you, the recruiter, can put in place a sourcing plan that will help you identify diverse candidates.

For a lower-level manager, entry level roles are often a quick-start. I can't tell you the number of companies with which I've worked that complained about diversity. "There is no diversity here," I'd often hear. Yet, a quick glance at the corporate directory told me that diversity was only a level or two away. Because there was plenty of diversity at the entry level. Often, however, there was no formalized way for the entry level folks to become introduced to the next step in the organization.

As a recruiter, you can tap into this pool to bring forward employees in entry level roles. Create an email list of first-level employees and send a list of appropriate positions on a regular basis. Make yourself available, either in 1:1

meetings or a regular group meeting to answer questions about requirements, interviewing and available positions. Help your managers reach employees by connecting your hiring manager with managers who lead entry level employees. Do whatever you can to help introduce entry-level staff and their managers to the next level up. Consult with the existing manager and keep a short list of employees – especially diverse employees – who may be ready to make a move. Ensure that these employees get opportunities to interview and be prepared to provide extra interview coaching as needed.

For some roles, at some companies, in certain locations, increasing the diversity of the team may prove more difficult and require even more planning. Sourcing diverse candidates often adds complexity, especially when the diversity that is needed is in short supply. For roles where racial diversity is required, the short supply could be due to location. Or perhaps the problem lies with the number of available candidates in the market. Finding female civil engineers, for example, might prove challenging, given that fewer than 17% of civil engineers are women. The numbers drop significantly when intersectionality is considered – if one wanted to add a black woman to a team of civil engineers, the number drops to .5%.[1]

From just this analysis it should be clear that adding diversity to a team is a complex set of problems to be solved. Often, it requires the help of senior leadership to set the tone and emphasize the importance of adding diversity to the team. Without this, diversifying the team becomes a sometimey activity. Easily done when diversity is plentiful, easily ignored when it is not. Your job as the recruiter is to help leadership and HR build a winnable strategy and secure support from senior execs before trying to execute that strategy.

You can help with this by providing an overall look at the data for your hiring leaders, understanding the existing diversity within the organization, the external numbers and by pinpointing the areas where you might achieve success. Starting the year, or the quarter, or your recruiting assignment, by having an in-depth conversation with the group leader to ascertain where emphasis

---

1 https://www.catalyst.org/research/women-in-male-dominated-industries-and-occupations/

and effort should be placed will help to focus your efforts and achieve diversity where it is needed most.

It is important to pull in your HR and Diversity team participants into this conversation. Once everyone has agreed on the kind of diversity the team most needs, and you have confirmed that the diversity does, indeed, exist, put together a plan of how you plan to achieve diversity goals within a reasonable time frame. You'll need to first confirm that the candidates you want exist, that the number of candidates exist, enough to meet your goals, and estimate the time it will take to find, engage, interview and hire these candidates.

It's also helpful to understand what your organization offers to these candidates, and areas where you are under-competitive. Recruiting black professionals to Seattle was a big challenge when I was a recruiter. There weren't many black people who lived there, and it was tough to form lasting networks. These days, if your company policy allows, there is no need to uproot people. They can telecommute, opening the sourcing floodgates, and making hiring racially diverse candidates somewhat easier.

If working from home is an option not available to you, and solving racial diversity is challenging, then sourcing becomes a long-term process. Outline the market to your managers and spend some time building a sourcing and recruitment marketing plan. Acknowledge the difficulty of attracting the diversity you need to your organization due to location and be realistic about how difficult it will be to attract candidates to your location. Build enough time in your plan and get started immediately! It is not impossible – you can find the candidates you need. But it will require time and effort. Work with your manager to make the position as attractive as possible and ready them to make the hire when the hire is ready. Not hiring a great diverse candidate because the manager doesn't have an open req is blasphemy!

If your challenge is recruiting for a profession where there are not enough diverse candidates in the pipeline or even available overall, then you are likely looking at an even longer sourcing project. As recommended above, work with your hiring manager/leader and HR to determine where to focus your efforts. Again, start with credible research on the talent market. How many diverse candidates are available, and where are they now? Are they senior in their organizations, mid- or early-career? Did many of them graduate from the same university program? Do candidates live in a certain part of the country? What do your talent competitors offer that you don't? What is critical to this group of talent? What can you offer that makes your organization attractive? You will have to answer these questions before reaching out to diverse candidates. You will have to know what their objections might be (they may not have any, they might simply be unaware of your company and opportunities), and be prepared to help candidates develop enthusiasm for your org. You must know both sides of the argument – why a diverse candidate would be wise to choose your organization and what about your organization encourages candidates to look elsewhere. You should be prepared to answer this question in its' broadest sense (why I should join Company X or move to Location Y), as well as its' the specifics about that specific job, market or hiring manager. Without having explored these questions and obtained answers, you will likely waste more time sourcing candidates who have little interest in your position or selling the wrong thing to the wrong candidate or simply wondering why your sourcing efforts failed.

Once you have gathered this data (see table below for an organized list), you must make some educated guesses on the number the candidates you will be able to attract, where (geographic location, current company) they are and how long it might take to hire the numbers you need. This is one of those areas where you earn your talent advisor stripes. You will have to guess, in the same way that your peers in sales, marketing or software development make guesses about what's needed, and the potential for success.

Below I've outlined the data you need to think clearly and deeply about your diversity recruiting strategy – what you need to know before you launch any initiatives.

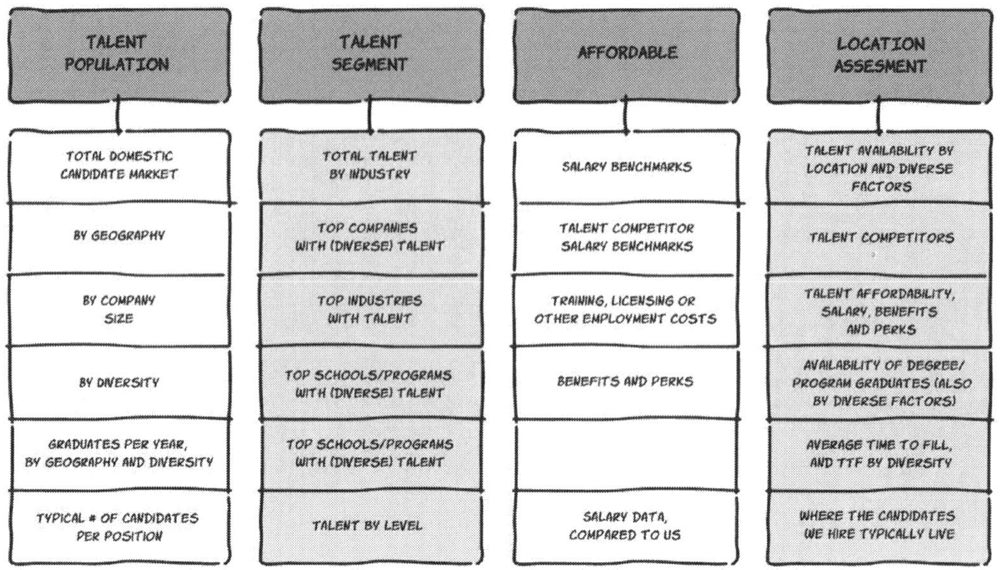

[Illustration 9]

In addition to understanding relevant data at your company, as well as the market and your talent competitors, it is important to help hiring managers understand the motivations of successful candidates. The easiest, most relevant place to find this kind of information is the existing team. Conduct a focus group (or interview individually) where you pose questions such as:

- what made them interested in your company?
- what keeps them interested?
- what is different at your company, compared to their previous company?
- what is different about the job that they like/dislike?
- what advice would you give to a candidate considering working here?
- and finally (of course) do they know others (especially diverse candidates) who might enjoy it as well? (Always be on the lookout for referrals!)

Armed with information about the market, the industry, salary and benefits, and location, as well as what candidates like and dislike about your organization, you can put together a strategy that has a chance of succeeding. Can you imagine what would happen if you didn't do this work first? I can. I have worked on quite a few ill- or under- informed diversity strategies that didn't track back to the actual market. Hire a ton of black developers in the Seattle market, without an informed strategy? A next to impossible job without understanding the existing talent market and having a clear understanding of the advantages and disadvantages of the opportunity for diverse candidates so that I could anticipate the candidate's needs and overcome objections where possible.

Lastly, ensure that your interview team is thoroughly prepped. What's most important is that they know how to select a qualified candidate, and that the interview team knows what skills, and what qualities, at what level is required. It is especially important to prep the interview team on the level of candidate you are seeking, or if you can be flexible with regard to leveling. It is not necessarily important to prep the team on diversity needs; it's most important that the interview team is able to evaluate candidates fairly.

Helping your organization diversify the employee base can be one of the greatest satisfactions of being a talent advisor. But step carefully. Do not agree to the task until you are sure that your hiring managers, their leaders, your HR partners have your back. With that kind of support, with numbers that back up your assertions, with a generous timeline and available reqs, you can achieve diversity goals in a reasonable time period. It takes some work, but you can help to ensure that our workplaces reflect the diversity of our customers, partners, and community. It is well worth the effort, imho.

TL;DR

- Share as much information about your company and your hiring process as possible.

- Get all the players (leadership, HR, hiring manager, sourcer, recruiter) involved in creating an achievable plan to increase diversity. Leverage data and be realistic!

- Self-reflect. Why would a candidate, or a diverse candidate, choose another organization over yours? Work to close the gap or provide an attractive alternative.

- Consider opening offices in different locations, work from home positions, internships, and any other arrangement that make you most attractive to all candidates

- Be certain that the interview team understands how to select for the position and are well-versed on the level of candidate you are seeking

Chapter 7 - Interviewing

I built an entire career of teaching managers and recruiters how to interview well. At the surface, "interviewing well" has many definitions. Ask any group of leaders if they're good at interviewing job candidates and they will say "of course – I've built fantastic teams!" But in further discussions they reveal just how little they know about interviewing, or perhaps they have knowledge in one area, but feel shaky in other areas. I often talk to tech leaders who have no idea how to identify whether candidates have the "soft skills" necessary to do a job well. They're great at assessing technical skills but fall short when it comes to identifying and screening candidates who have the competencies necessary to get work done in their specific environment. It is important that hiring managers are great at assessing technical skills and behavioral skills. Do not let them convince you to separate the process and have some people focus on technical and others focus on behavioral skills.

As the recruiter, you have several structural pieces that you can put in place to ensure that candidates are interviewed well and fairly, and appropriately, deeply assessed. It all goes right back to the hiring criteria the manager shared in the very first meeting. Ensure that the hiring manager still believes they have set the right criteria, both hard skills and "soft skills" or competencies, against which every candidate will be assessed. This is an important step. I've seen so many recruiting processes go off the rails because the hiring manager isn't certain or doesn't remember or has changed their mind about their needs. Everyone needs to be aligned and in agreement.

Once you have achieved alignment with the hiring manager, you must ensure that the interviewers are similarly aligned. Set up a short meeting with (or send a detailed email to) the entire interviewing team to review the hiring criteria, skills and competencies, outline the process and timing, remind the interview team to provide a great candidate experience, and answer any questions. Teams that have worked together frequently don't need as much handholding, but teams where there are several new interviewers or interviewing teams that have not worked together in the past might require more time. Encourage discussion, so that everyone leaves with a clear and shared understanding of hiring criteria. The last thing that you want is to have an interview team – each with their own idea of what it means to land the job – assessing the candidate in different ways, drawing a myriad of conclusions, unable to make a reasonable decision about the candidate's ability to contribute.

The hiring manager should own this discussion and listen carefully to the questions asked by the team. Ensure that the manager adequately explains the need, explains the candidate skills and competencies in a 'good-better-best' format so that everyone is on the same page. This is perhaps the most overlooked, but critically important, stage of the interviewing process. Sending your hiring team out to interview without knowing why they're interviewing is a sure-fire way to ensure a mixed review of the candidate, with every party uncertain if the candidate should be hired.

You or the hiring manager will likely want to review the hard skills required, as well as the soft skills necessary to do the job well. Be prepared to outline the soft skills; what does the hiring manager mean when they say the candidate must be "creative" or "loves to solve complex problems" or "has a sense of ownership." If the group is not well-versed on what each soft skill means, now is the time to review, share reference materials, and ensure that the interview team is aligned on exactly what it is they are interviewing for. Without this kind of deep alignment, you will waste a lot of time interviewing and arguing about whether a candidate brings what you need to the table. Every candidate brings something. The question is whether it is what you need. And the definition of what you need is the stabilizing factor that allows you to make decisions quickly, with confidence. Be clear about what those skills and competencies are, and the depth to which you need them, and interviewing and assessing candidates becomes so much easier.

Another area to ensure gets covered during the alignment meeting is candidate level. The manager should make clear the level of the candidate that will be hired and set the expectation that interviewers should try to ascertain the candidate's actual experience level, as well as the candidate's ability and timeline to ascend to the next level. If there is wiggle room to assess and adjust the level of the position, let your interviewers know. The goal is both to uncover a position that fits the candidate's skills, as well as hire the right person for the job.

If you find that your interviewing team returns with mixed results, or always finds themselves settling for a "middle of the road" candidate rating, it's likely because the recruiter and the hiring manager have not done the work to prep interviewers for the candidates to come.

As the recruiter, you will want to remind the team that you are assessing each candidate against the criteria – the skills and competencies – that have been set, not against the skills and competencies of other candidates. It is, perhaps, human nature to want to judge each candidate against the other candidates, beauty pageant style, but it is not the best way to build a diverse, high-performing team. I've seen hiring teams that interviewed an unqualified candidate become enthralled with a slightly less unqualified candidate. In the end, both candidates shouldn't have made the cut.

Your job, as a talent advisor, is to ensure that the entire team feels confident enough to make a decision. "Maybe" doesn't count. Each interviewer should walk away feeling confident voting yea or nay, based on what they were assigned to cover during the interview. Interviewers that consistently pick a middle vote either haven't been prepared or have failed to put in the work required to interview successfully. Again, this is where you get to earn your stripes as a talent advisor. If interview training is necessary, then alert the hiring manager and get the help needed. If the interviewer merely failed to interview well, you might suggest that this person either get some coaching, training, shadow more expert interviewers or not be part of the interview team!

A bit more about the interview team. They need your help. They are aware that they are making an important decision. It's your job, as a talent advisor, to ensure that they are making that important decision based on the right criteria.

If your interview teams are anything like the people I have met in my years of leading recruiting and consulting to businesses who want to improve recruiting, then they are likely fuzzy about how to make the decision. This means that you must design an interview process that makes sense, that helps interviewers assess the right skills and behaviors.

Often, interview teams will insert exercises or tests, if you will, to determine if a candidate has the correct skills. Insert yourself here to 1) ensure that the exercise or test does indeed measure the skill that interviewers wish to assess and 2) that the assessment is fair, easy to understand, legal, is not biased and doesn't overburden the candidate. It's also important to ensure that when assessing the candidate, this instrument does not take an outsized position. Ensure that interviewers keep in mind that the exercise is only one part of what's needed to assess the candidate. Remind them that often, the reasons a new hire isn't successful is not related to testable skills. It is often their "soft skills" or behaviors or competencies that is at the root of failure, so the ability to assess their responses to common situations, their communication style and *the way they work* is as important as *what they know*. Putting too much emphasis on exercises and tests obscures perhaps the most important information that interviewers gather during the interview process.

Once you are satisfied that your interviewers are assessing the right skills and behaviors, once you feel certain that they will interview for both skills and behaviors, and once you are assured that everyone knows how to do this, it's time to invite your first candidate to interview. If you are working with a new team, you may want to put a bit of time between the first interview and subsequent candidates. You will want to ensure that all went well with the first candidate, that decisions can easily be made, that adjustments aren't necessary.

Ensure that your interviewers know what to do and when to do it. If you expect them to write their notes and immediately make a decision after each interview, set this expectation and ensure that your ATS is configured to work this way. My preference is that interviewers get feedback in the system within 24 hours. I know some recruiting leaders that have a same workday policy. The point here is that the longer interviewers allow feedback to marinate, the less reliable it becomes.

A note here, dear Talent Advisor. Please ensure that your entire hiring team knows how to review candidates, submit feedback and use your ATS system. I recommend a monthly or quarterly call where you share the most important bits and follow up with a supporting document and assurances that you and your team are always available to help or even provide a smaller, more in-depth and specific training.

Submitting feedback is often easier than interviewers believe. Especially if you have assigned focus areas to each interviewer, and the interviewer is well versed on the skills, the level, and the behaviors needed to do well at the job. Remind interviewers that you are looking for an unequivocal yes or no that can be explained clearly in a sentence or two. Interviewers are often relieved when they realize that you don't need long paragraphs of candidate feedback. But this requires that they have a solid understanding of what they are looking for in the first place. They are also relieved when they realize that the entire decision is not left up to them. That they are interviewing for a few key skills and behaviors and their initial assessment should be based on those items. Only after hearing the results from the other interviewers will they be invited to help make the final decision.

Another bite-sized training opportunity is helping interviewers write feedback. Set up a lunch-and-learn where you share your tips on how to efficiently capture what's important, what to write (and what to leave to discussion) and how to make a decision. Do this twice a year. You will be surprised by what you learn. Add value!

Lastly, prepare your interviewers to provide a great candidate experience. Make sure they understand what this means, and their role. To smile and be welcoming to every candidate. To ensure that the candidate – no matter the decision – walks away feeling as if the interviews were fair, that they walked away with a good idea of what the team wanted to accomplish, and how this role would contribute. It is a good idea to assign this matter to one of the first interviewers. Ensure that one of the first interviewers describe to the candidate the role and the expectations of the person in the role. Let the candidate know that they are competing with a few other candidates who are as experienced and talented, and that your decision will be based on the experience, skills, and competencies that they might bring to the position. Often, candidates don't remember that interviewing is a competitive sport. A gentle reminder might make the candidate more competitive, and at the very least, a reminder that they were in a competitive situation might ease the pain of not getting the position, if that time comes.

Remind all interviewers to leave time for candidate questions, and to note those questions. Often, we learn about the experience we're providing, as well as the experience level, the interest level, the particular interests and aspirations of the candidate based on the questions they ask.

At this stage, you become a troubleshooter. Fixing schedules that have fallen apart, ensuring that interviewers have what they need and that they're prepared, ensuring that your candidates know what to expect. Things will go wrong. It's inevitable. Like the time the recruiting coordinator invited a candidate to fly in from the east coast for interviews. Candidate arrives, is excited, in the lobby. I find out a few minutes later that no schedule has been set with their interviewers. So the candidate was there, in the lobby, *with no scheduled interviews*. That was a bit of a scramble. Or there was the time a young woman grew warm in an interview and removed her top layer. Only, she removed a second, and sole remaining, layer at the same time. Luckily, I was there to talk the interviewer down from the cliff from which he was surely going to jump! Or the time a candidate called me to let me know that the interview team had asked some very private and illegal questions. She promised that she wasn't going to sue – this time – but I'd better do something about them before someone did sue. I quickly got the manager (and his leader) on board and set up interview training. After many years of delivering interview training, I can assure you that many (most?) managers do not know enough about what's legal and what's not allowed during interviews!

If you've been recruiting for any amount of time, you can likely match me story for story. This is when we earn the donuts. If we're lucky, we can spot what's needed a mile away and prevent it from happening. If not, if we're in the moment, then it's our job to fix things for now and to figure out how to prevent them from happening again. If you have leadership on your mind, perhaps this is something you can fix for your entire organization or company. Perhaps these kinds of surprises are why I find recruiting such an interesting job. You never know what will be needed. You need to be quick on your feet. You must take things in stride (at least outwardly) and you must help your team realize the best immediate and long-term outcome.

The thing about being a talent advisor is that you must approach every day with an appreciation for the unknown. The surefire candidate that pulls out at the last second. The hiring manager who insists on hiring the least talented candidate. The interviewer who forgets to share his notes in a timely fashion. The big "no" from the comp team when it comes to increasing the salary even though the market for top talent is burning hot. Your job is to make it all work, at every level, every day. You've gotta be organized, yet not so rigid as to discourage discussion and change as necessary. In many cases, you deliver 5x as many "no hires" as celebratory high fives. Yet you've got to remain in the game. I think recruiting is one of those jobs that you must love to do in order to retain your sanity. It takes a special personality to do this well and to fall in love with it. You will lose on some days. You will get it wrong on others. But you will remember – for the rest of your life – those days you got it right. I still remember the smiles and hugs from the candidates that I helped to place in the perfect job. Nothing beats it!

Interviewing - A Few Parting Words

I've said on many occasions that recruiting isn't rocket science. You don't have to be terribly brilliant to do it well. It's more like a high-wire act. You've got to be skilled, your supporting equipment and process must be solid and you should be prepared to deal with unforeseen emergencies (i.e., high winds, or hiring managers who change their minds).

That said, the profession is on the cusp of change. We're seeing artificial intelligence worm its way into the way we do business. And recruiting is at the forefront of this change. We've seen major employers lay off thousands of recruiters, perhaps with the hope that AI will take their place. I won't make any predictions; it's too early to declare the death of the corporate recruiter or predict major shifts in the way that we work. But here are some things I know:

- We can't predict success. We can try. But humanity is at the root of what we do, and to accurately predict success requires access to past and future behavior predictors that the interview process does not currently afford us.

- Recruiting well is still a slow process. When I started in this business, the average time to hire remains about the same. There are many reasons for this, but you'd think with the introduction of technology, things would have improved a bit. Our businesses are growing impatient. They are looking ways to speed up and improve the process. AI will likely be critical to success, so it's important that we jump right in the fray.

- The skills required to do a great job are changing. We are used to assessing for base skills – math and computation, communication skills, the ability to use certain tools, for example. We are moving into a world where expectations are growing because the machines can do the base work for us. We will likely be asked to help managers more deeply define role expectations and performance standards, and this will change the profile of who can be successful in each role. As recruiters, we should get ahead of this.

- Recruiting for talent used to be a local activity. At most, for senior roles, we'd consider relocating talent. That is rapidly changing. Sure, some companies are clinging to the 'you must come into the office' model. But many companies (especially the smaller ones, looking for an advantage in the talent market) have happily extended the work from home model. Saving themselves great expenses and increasing their access to diverse talent across the country. Expand that to increasing access to talent globally and we are in a whole new ballgame!

Perhaps you are not close enough to the decisions at the top and find it hard to see change coming your way. That doesn't mean you shouldn't keep tabs on what's happening at your company, in your market, in your vertical and in general. As a recruiter with some vision into the external market and into the hiring practices of your competitors, your understanding is often as solid as the understanding of the managers you help.

TL;DR

- Before interviewing begins, ensure that you, the hiring manager and the interviewers are aligned on the hard skills and soft skills required of the successful candidate. Understand the need so deeply that you can easily describe what the successful candidate has done, and what they will be able to achieve in your environment

- Don't accept middle-of-the-road decisions. A candidate is either "no hire" or "can't wait until they're onboard". In between candidates may have some great traits, but they aren't yet ready, which makes them a "no hire"

- Get everyone involved in ensuring the candidate has a great experience

Chapter 8 - Post-Interview, Decision Making and Compensation

I suppose the first thing to discuss here is the timing of decisions about candidates and the decision to hire. I view these as two different decision points. Make decisions about individual candidates immediately – as quickly as possible – and communicate to your candidates quickly. By the end of the week you likely have a list of candidates about whom you have collected feedback and decisions. Don't shut down your computer until you have communicated decisions or next steps to each candidate.

So how do you get your interview team to make decisions quickly? My first piece of advice is to schedule interview debriefs, per candidate, as quickly as possible following the interview. Same day, if possible. Schedule the debrief meeting at the same time – or just after -- you schedule the interview. If an interviewer cannot participate in the candidate debrief meeting, then they cannot interview the candidate. The reason I suggest a meeting per candidate, vs debriefing about all the candidates at once, is that a single meeting per candidate helps interviewers focus, prevents interviewers from comparing candidates, helps interviewers have clearer discussions about the candidate's fitness for the job and it allows the clearest, fastest communication from you to the candidate. Preserving clear feedback and memory and working quickly to disposition candidates are other benefits of doing it this way.

If your team objects and wants to debrief all the candidates at once, you will have to ensure that the debrief meeting is run in an exacting fashion so that each candidate gets due attention and to ensure that the decision is made by comparing each candidate to the criteria, over comparing candidates to each other. A meeting to discuss a single candidate can run as little as 10-15 minutes. If you are meeting to discuss all 3-4 candidates, I'd put an hour on the calendar to ensure enough time.

How should a debrief meeting be structured? There are several models, but this is my favorite:

1. Recruiter hosts meeting, starts off by restating the skills and qualities needed to be successful. All interviewers have submitted feedback, but this feedback is only shared with the recruiter and the hiring manager.

2. Each interviewer shares hire/no hire decision based on what they were assigned to cover and shares additional info that led them to their decision. Leader or manager goes last, to encourage less experienced team members to fully contribute.

3. Interviewers entertain Q&A, hiring manager ensures that the interviews covered all of the skills and competencies required, and leads a spirited debate if the decision to hire or not hire is unclear. The team votes again, based on everything they have heard during the debrief.

4. Recruiter confirms the vote, calls for questions that need to be answered and confirms next steps with the hiring manager. In most organizations, the hiring manager gets the final say, but makes decisions in accordance to what was heard from the entire interview team.

A word about feedback. This is where you, the recruiter, must pay close attention to the discussion and assess whether the team interviewed thoroughly and fairly. Make sure the feedback being shared is related to the skills and competencies originally stated, and if it becomes clear that something got missed, that a new skill or competency gets added, that element is included when debriefing all candidates. Probably worth a quick discussion with the hiring manager, asking if this new skill or behavior is essential to hiring the right candidate.

Managers and interviewers might not see how unfair the process becomes when a candidate is different than members of the team. When, for example, a female candidate is judged more severely for communication style than male candidates. Or a new skill, one that didn't show up during the alignment meeting suddenly becomes critically important. It's your job – as the recruiter – to double check the importance of the skill (and to make changes to the profile, and sometimes, to start the search over). Often, the skill is not critical to being the successful candidate, it is something that is favored by one of the interviewers, or something that can be learned on the job. This is where we earn the donuts, ensuring that the process is fair and reasonable, ensuring that the right decision gets made, ensuring that the process runs smoothly and fairly for every candidate.

Another pitfall during the decision meeting is the strong desire to rate candidates in the middle of the road. The "she's OK, so let's just hire her" approach. Managers, if you are looking to build a strong team, I highly recommend that you reject this approach. I have helped many recruiting leaders build rating systems for candidates; I strongly advise against a 3- or 5-point rating scale. That middle rating is there only to satisfy the interviewer who isn't confident enough to make a decision. I say build the muscle and force interviewers to strongly support hiring a candidate, or to say no when the candidate misses the mark.

This advice is tough for interviewers, especially those new to the game. But giving your interviewers permission to say 'no' (instead of 'maybe' or "OK, if others are OK with hiring them") is critical if your organization wants to build strong teams. I recommend that recruiters help their teams make solid decisions and normalize 'no'. If you can't get rid of the middle of the road feedback system, get rid of middle of the road voting. Normalize resounding yeses and confident nos. Get interviewers to admit that their 'maybes' are votes for nice, likeable people, not a vote to hire someone onto the team. Once, I even clarified things for the team by getting them to vote twice. The first vote, I asked who thought the candidate was a fantastic communicator and would be fun to have around. The second vote was whether or not the candidate should be hired to do the job. The interview team laughed, but they got it – not every nice person will have the skills and qualities to do the job.

Of course, the recruiter is on the hook for delivering the "no" message. It's not always easy to do. I firmly believe that if a candidate set aside time to meet with people in my company, then communication of the decision should be live, not in an email. Set up a time to discuss the decision in advance. I set a time on my schedule every week to deliver "no" to candidates. Your options:

- "We enjoyed meeting with you and thought you had several great qualities. However, we are looking for someone with more experience in ______ and have decided to go with another candidate."

- "We enjoyed meeting with you, and I am happy to report that you are one of 2 top candidates. Our final step is ____. We will make a decision quickly after that."

I tried to prepare candidates for "No" throughout the process by reminding them that they were competing for the role, even if I had pursued them, even if I had encouraged them to apply. (I also prep them for 'Yes' – especially when things are looking good – by asking pointed questions about making a solid offer, about their work environment preferences, etc.)

When rejecting a candidate, I did three things. First, I delivered the message quickly and clearly up front. Second, I offered a small bit of feedback and offered to go more deeply into feedback – if they wished – at a later time. Third, I got their permission to reach out should another role come up. These calls usually lasted 5 minutes or so.

Typically, candidates hearing 'no' need time to compose themselves and their thoughts and questions. Believe me, lengthy discussions at this stage are fruitless. The candidate isn't prepared to hear your feedback, and any discussion is likely an argument for why you're making the wrong decision. But it is an argument they cannot win, and one you don't want to have. So, if the candidate insists, schedule a time at a later date to share more specific feedback. That way, they have time to process the rejection and you have time to gather and deliver useful feedback.

Making offers is the fun part of the job. It can also be the most fretful part of the job if you don't set yourself up for success. My advice is to start at the very beginning – during your first discussions with the hiring manager – to devise the right comp strategy. Remember, it's not just about what your manager/company is willing to pay. The equation also includes what the candidate is willing to accept, non-monetary comp, the level of candidate that your dollars will buy, the position level the candidate is willing to accept, the going rate at your competitors and a hundred more parts of the equation.

Do your very best to determine current comp, or the market rate for this position, especially at talent competitors and have that discussion with your hiring manager right away. What will you do if your comp is low? Downgrade the position? Lobby for more money? Take your chances (which will likely slow the process)? All of these are acceptable approaches. It's important to agree on a plan and next steps before you reach the decision point.

Upon first talking to the candidate, have the initial discussion about comp. I live in Seattle, where it is illegal to base comp for the role on the candidate's existing comp (thus, recruiters cannot ask "what is your current compensation?"). Instead, ask the candidate the salary they would find acceptable for the role described. Smart candidates won't answer that question, and instead will ask you what is the range for this position? In Washington state, you'd better be prepared to answer to stay in accordance with the law. And many states are following. Colorado, Washington, California and New York have passed similar laws. Why? Because in the past, women faced discrimination in compensation, often being paid less than males doing the very same job (it happened to me in the early 2000's at a Fortune 200 company!). This pay discrimination would follow the (often female or minority) candidate for the rest of their career (and thus continue the pattern of underpayment) if salaries continued to be based on the first discriminatory salary. In fact, my opinion on how this discussion should be handled changed as a result of this law. The discussion should start with the recruiter stating the salary range and ask if the range fits with the candidate's expectations. That's much more respectful, less antagonistic way to start. The recruiter explains the range – that candidates with more relevant experience may be offered more, and that the candidate will have the opportunity to improve their salary over time.

Having secured the candidate's salary or range, you're in a much better position to craft an offer that will delight the candidate. If the candidate is on the high end of your range, yet their skills place them solidly in the mid-range or below, you'll have adequate time to prepare the candidate and help them adjust their expectations, as well as work with the hiring manager to do what you can to make the very best offer without displacing their entire team. In the area of salary negotiations, we walk the high wire! Sometimes we fight for our candidates to squeeze the last available dime out of the org, and sometimes we must stand up for the org, become deft, tough (but likeable) negotiator on behalf of the company. The key is to know when we must take a hard line to support the candidate or the company. In most cases, if you start with an honest conversation about salary expectations, if you share a fair range with the candidate, if you add a little surprise and delight at the end (in the form of salary, bonus, time off, or a particularly attractive benefit), you will have no problem closing your candidate. To do this, you must discuss compensation at the very beginning of the process, understand what's important to the candidate and set realistic expectations. You must do this on multiple occasions and assess the candidate's excitement about the likely offer throughout the process, to avoid nasty surprises at the end.

In my day (whew, I am old enough to say that!) it was rare to have a candidate reject my offer, especially if I had done my due diligence, prepared the candidate, and gauged their excitement to join the team. But times have changed. Candidates have become savvier and have more resources to find out exactly what they should get in an offer from you. A well-formed question to ChatGPT, or a LinkedIn search or Levels.fyi reveals information that is accurate enough. That's why transparency, from the very beginning, a good understanding of what the candidate will – and will not – accept is the best way to close deals.

Make sure that you have pre-closed the candidate on all factors of the new job – not just money – before making a formal offer. Check in with the candidate on

- Their motivation – what's driving them to look for a new position, or what excites them about finding a new role? This role? Reiterate how that will show up in their new job at your company.

- Job Content – does the job offer enough different day-to-day responsibilities? Will they learn new systems or approaches? Will they be responsible for different or larger areas? Will they have exciting opportunities? Ensure that the hiring manager emphasizes this during their conversations.

- Impact – how will their work matter to the team, to the company? Make sure a few of the team members share this during the interviews.

- Career Growth – will this opportunity lead to growth and new opportunities? Will the manager/company take a stake in allowing the candidate to (formally or informally) learn more, take on more responsibilities? Make sure the manager addresses this with the candidate.

- Their timeline – how soon are they willing to resign from their current position. How soon will they be able to start? (Giving the candidate a couple of weeks to decompress and take a vacation is a nice, non-comp perk to add if needed)

- Counter-offer/Competition – what will they do when their current company makes a competitive offer for them to stay? It's a good idea to coach them through this conversation. *"It's likely your manager will make a counter-offer right after you resign. I only ask that you not accept on the spot. Let's have a conversation about it. I don't think we're talking solely because you want a bigger salary."*

It's also important to know if the candidate is expecting (or has received) offers from other companies. It's not uncommon for a candidate, once they've stuck their toe in the market, decides to stick their foot into it. Staying close to your candidate in this situation is your best defense. Knowing your competitor and putting a human face on all parts of the process is the key to "winning." I'm a big fan of all out honesty in this case as well. If a candidate gets another, better offer, moneywise, say so. "I don't think we can compete with an offer that lucrative, to be honest. I think this position will offer better career trajectory, but I wouldn't stand in the way of such an impressive number." I've had more than one candidate say no to a higher offer because they felt my company was more invested in their career! For more excellent advice on closing the deal, I highly recommend reading or listening to *Never Split the Difference* by Chris Voss. The book is an interesting look at how an FBI negotiator breaks down deals and delivers win-win solutions in highly charged situations. I enjoyed the read and learned a lot about human nature and negotiation.

Closing the candidate becomes everyone's responsibility. There is nothing like the feeling of a team eagerly awaiting your arrival! It makes a huge difference if a candidate understands how much they are needed by the team!

Yet few teams get this right. I have even walked into hostile situations, as a new leader, for which I was not prepared. The hiring manager (my leader) failed to tell the team that I, new to the company, was taking on the role as the new manager, despite several on the team who interviewed for the position. My leader should have made it clear why I was chosen over the internals and perhaps smoothed the way for me a bit. A lesson for hiring managers, especially those entertaining team members and other internal candidates. Be prepared to thoroughly explain the job's required skills and qualities, so that you can easily explain why the winning candidate won, and what those who didn't get the job must develop in order to someday get there.

Once you have sealed the deal and secured a "yes" from the candidate, there are a few steps left. The first is to ensure that the candidate, now new employee, is scheduled and set up for a well-designed on-boarding. Many organizations have defined programs, but it might be helpful to think about what was important to the candidate and set up a few side meetings that might be helpful.

Don't forget the post-recruiting process review. You will want to meet with the hiring manager to determine what went well during the search, and what could have gone better. Don't forget to address the needs of interviewers. Were they good at assessing skills? Do they need additional help writing feedback? What about sourcing – what did you learn during the process that might be helpful should the manager have a similar opening in the future. This kind of follow up increases learning for you and the hiring manager and places you squarely in the category of talent advisor!

Additionally, set up a check-in meeting, about a month after the candidate arrives, to ensure that they are enjoying the new job and work environment, to find out if anything was missed during orientation, to discover if there is some way you can be helpful as they slide into the new work environment. And of course, to collect any referrals they may have!

TL:DR

- Make decisions about candidates as quickly as possible; remember to compare candidates to the criteria you set, not to other candidates.

- Set yourself up for success from the first conversation with the candidate. Share the salary range for the job and confirm with the candidate that the range fits with their expectations. Continue to collect information about salary, career aspirations, what makes them happy at work along the way.

- Pre-close the winning candidate before presenting the final offer. Capture all the information needed to create a compelling offer and be certain that the candidate will accept before presenting a written offer.

- Get the hiring manager, and perhaps the hiring team, involved in closing the deal. Candidates love it when their new employer showers them with attention!

End Note for Recruiters

That's all I have for you, recruiters. As I stated, I doubt that all of this is new to you. But I do hope you were able to glean a few tips that might have been missing or forgotten. As I write this, we are on the eve of learning how artificial intelligence will change what we do. Every prominent tool is under transformation. I believe that certain recruiting organizations are already thinking about how they will use these powerful tools to enhance, sourcing and selection. Recruiters might be afraid of what this means for them – does it mean that we become extinct? I don't think so. I think it means that we become better at what we do best – helping managers select top talent.

I am especially hopeful that as AI helps us find top talent, we get better at helping managers think about and select the most appropriate talent for their teams and for the job. If my vision gets realized, recruiters will be experts at coaxing the parameters of the skills and qualities from managers, translating that for AI, and reviewing and refining the search results. I think this gets us improved time-to-till results. Even more importantly, this gets us a better chance to find new employees that slide quite happily into our organizations, perform at their best and help our companies realize their goals. That's what I think. We'll soon see.

Part II –
Going Deeper: For Recruiting Leaders and High-Performing Recruiters

Leading a recruiting team is a full-contact sport. To do it well, I think you must be engaged at four levels. You must first deeply understand the businesses you support, and their recruiting needs. This might be simple (you manage a team of recruiters for a single org, with well-defined and understood business objectives, or it might be more complex (you lead recruiting for a large part of the business, each business unit with different objectives and at a different stage of growth and a large team of recruiters, specialists, recruiting managers or leaders, with varying skills and skill levels.)

Secondly, you must build and foster a recruiting team that can perform at the level of sophistication needed for the business(es). This means you must balance 1) understanding what your business needs 2) understanding how to build and grow a recruiting team 3) understanding the talent market for recruiters and 4) providing development for recruiters, based on the capabilities, needs and desires of your organization.

Third, you must build and measure the operational processes that your org requires. Everything from managing the requisition process, ensuring that it is easy to stop, start and continue as needed, to managing the employee referral process, to determining the tools needed by the recruiting team to perform at a high level, to leveraging the internal recruiting process to meet hiring needs, increase efficiency and keep your talent happy, to ensuring that you're able to build and leverage an employer brand in order to attract the best candidates possible.

And fourth, you must develop and manage the relationship between recruiting and the client groups that recruiting supports. You must ensure that leaders, hiring managers and employees understand the services you provide, where and how to access them, and ensure that your work supports the goals of the businesses you support.

If you're able to nail these four areas, you're well on your way to being a best-in-class recruiting leader. Let's dive a little deeper into each area.

Chapter 9 - Determining the Needs of the Businesses You Support

You've just landed a recruiting leader/manager/director role. The team is performing its job, as they understand it, to the best of their abilities. But you know that corporate leadership isn't entirely happy. They realize that the recruiting team is working hard, but there is misalignment. It's your job to figure out what's broken and fix it, asap. What do you do? Time to build a plan.

You will want to first put into place the set of KPIs, Key Performance Indicators, that will drive your work. As the TA leader, your job is to understand your organization, where it wants to go, how it likes to get things done. It's also your job to understand the talent market, the constraints you're bound by, and what important changes you must make to best serve the organization. It's possible that KPIs already exist for TA. If not, you will have to first understand what your organization needs from recruiting. Your org might just need to keep the trains running on time – you're getting the talent you need; you just need to make sure that talent acquisition is efficient. Or, your organization might need to uplevel talent, in anticipation of market changes. Or there's been a shift in the talent market, your organization has more talent competitors, and you need to compete more fiercely. You get the drift.

Whatever the case, you will want to set your KPIs; the comparative business metrics that will help you and business leaders track success, the metrics that you will use to measure the success of your team, the level of performance that you want to achieve. I don't recommend setting KPIs in a vacuum. These should be set once you have gathered input and approval from leadership.

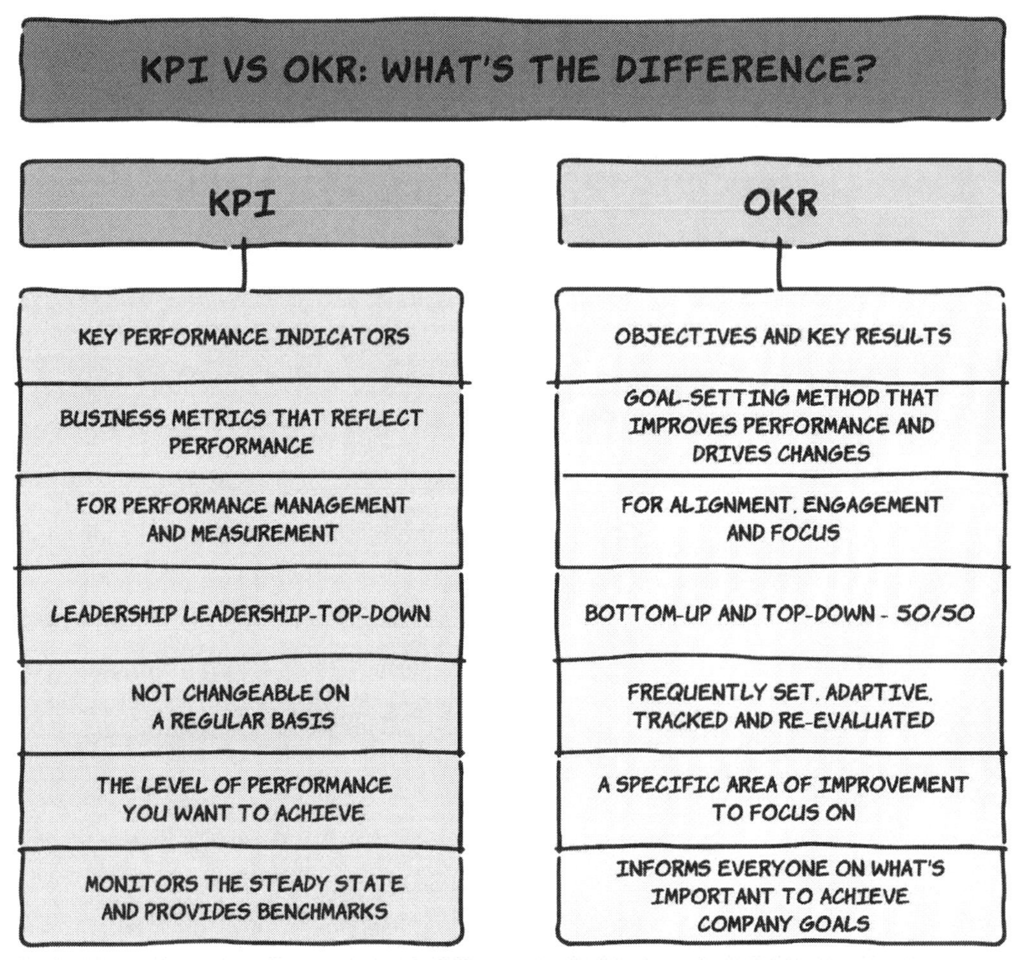

[Illustration 10]

After you have set your KPIs, it's time to work with your team to tackle the Objectives and Key Results (OKRs). The first thing is to figure out what's working, and what's not working at three levels. The Leadership Level, The Hiring Manager Level and the Recruiter Level. These are your three constituencies and I guarantee that there is misalignment with at least two of these groups, if not all three, at some level, on some topic, in your org. You're only going to find this out by talking to folks (and perhaps combining those conversations with some polls), digging into existing internal and external data and relying on what you know to design the best strategy to get done what needs to be done.

What's more, once you figure it out, you'll have to start again, if you're with the same organization. The strategy to get the organization the talent it needs changes. Quite frequently. A sudden shift in the market might make it more difficult to attract the talent you need. Or the business decides to pull back on one product and decides to promote another, which changes everything from the type of sales force needed, to the type of engineering and marketing talent to your ability to compete in the talent market. Or a million other scenarios. Your job, as recruiting leader, is to stay on top of the change, maybe even get ahead of it if you can, and implement the changes in staff, process and tools to keep your organization running the way it should. You will always feel uneasy about the way things are going. If that's true, you know you're doing a great job!

I learned my lesson when I was at Yahoo! When suddenly a group that I supported couldn't get the talent at the level it needed. There were new companies and startups in the mix that were usurping the talent that Y! was used to easily recruiting. The strategy -- and some of the recruiters -- needed to change. Where it was once easy to attract the needed talent, the market had become crowded with great employers, many of which were perceived as more exciting, more interesting technically, than Yahoo! After many discussions with leaders, managers, teams, individual recruiters, external and internal branding experts and external talent, we decided to address our reputation via a re-branding. We went from "How Big Can You Think" to "Think Big. Think Purple." We changed the look and feel of Yahoo employer branding to help potential candidates understand the scale at which we worked (big), and as a preview into a bit of our unique quirkiness (purple). We supported our rebranding with a host of other activities, including a revamped employee referral program, and internal events and communications to help employees understand and share the message.

This rebranding effort intersected with other efforts to increase technical hires, including the referral program, fixing backend systems, direct sourcing, measuring what was and wasn't working and other pieces of the puzzle I have likely long since forgotten. We recognized what we needed to do, and the order in which we needed to accomplish things only by first talking with our teams, understanding, and confirming the problems, creating a plan, reconfirming that we were on the right track and then executing. The most important parts of this story were rooted in the conversations we had across the board.

So how do you get started? Before you dive into a strategy, you must first be very clear about your objectives. To take an approach or a project without first deeply understanding the need and urgency for your organization is likely a big mistake, and can cost you precious time, dollars and, most importantly, your reputation.

Start with informal conversations with three groups:

- Leadership – Find out what they're happy about, and what's unsatisfactory for them. Delve into their view of the future, and how that compares to the current staffing model. Find out what questions are most important to them, from a recruiting standpoint, and find out whether they are getting the answers they need. Get examples. Tell them what you're up to but make only one promise at this beginning stage: promise to find out what's happening and report back. It's too early to promise change until you have the complete picture.

- Hiring Managers – Find out if the recruiting team is meeting their hiring needs. If so, what, specifically, is keeping them happy? Have they seen the org change, and what are the benefits of the change? If they're not happy, dig into what isn't working and their ideas about what it would take to improve the situation. Have they looked at the profiles for which they recruit and compared the profiles to what's available in the market? Are they aware of changes to the way they do business? Will their current teams support future needs? Again, this isn't the time to make promises. Remind them that you're on a quest to figure out what change is needed and that you will be back for a second round, and you will certainly be back to get their sign-off on the necessary changes.

- Recruiters – Your job here is to understand the level at which the recruiting team is performing, if they need help, and if you think they should be performing differently. Do they have the tools they need to get the job done? Do they have the support of hiring managers and leaders? Are they viewed as fast and capable? Do they have opportunities to advance both within and outside of recruiting? Are they recognized for their contributions?

Take a second pass at understanding the overall TA needs of the organization, this time from a 360° viewpoint. Sketch a model for your ideal TA org, taking into account the need to address the issues you have uncovered. Move people around, if required. Figure out if the team you currently have will be the same team that delivers results for hiring managers. Consider the training needed, formal and informal, to deliver what's needed.

After you have collected this information, you can begin to build broad strategies for each client group. Here's an example of a format I like to summarize the needs of a team:

TEAM/ROLE: FINANCIAL ANALYSTS (14 OPEN POSITIONS)	CURRENT STATE	CHANGE/NEEDS	PRIORITY
JOB DESCRIPTIONS	NOT FOCUSED ON THE JOB; TOO MUCH CORPORATE LANGUAGE	• UPDATE JD INPUT TOOL, • CREATE SAMPLE JDS • TRAIN RECRUITERS	B
SYSTEM/TOOLS	CURRENT PRIMARY SOURCE NOT PRODUCING GREAT CANDIDATES	• EXPLORE NEW TOOLS • ENGAGE AGENCY TO ASSIST WITH SOURCING	B
SOURCING STRATEGY/ SOURCING QUALITY	AGENCY CANDIDATES PREFERRED	• UPDATE CANDIDATE PRESENTATION • CREATE CANDIDATE PRESENTATION STANDARDS AND TRAINING FOR RECRUITERS	B
CANDIDATE QUALITY	QUALITY FALLING OFF	SEE ABOVE	B
INTERVIEW PROCESS	TOO MANY INTERVIEWERS	• TRAIN RECRUITERS TO HELP MANAGERS DECREASE LOOPS • INTERVIEW AND DECISION-MAKING TRAINING FOR MANAGERS	A
DECISION-MAKING	SLOW OR NO DECISION	SEE ABOVE	A
OFFER: ACCEPT	FEWER CANDIDATES ACCEPTING OFFERS	• ANALYZE OFFERS, UNDERSTAND WHERE WE STAND IN THE MARKET	B
ONBOARDING	NEW HIRES NOT FAMILIAR WITH COMPANY	• CREATE PRE-START MATERIALS KIT • UPDATE ONBOARDING PRESO • ENSURE RECRUITERS CHECK IN WITH NEW HIRES	C

[Illustration 11]

It's important to work with recruiting managers or the top recruiter for each group as you're completing this work. A second pair of eyes will keep you focused on the right strategies and secondly, this is a fantastic opportunity for someone on your team to develop leadership skills.

It's also important to review all the summaries to discover patterns. If time spent sourcing is problematic for several large groups, perhaps it is time to execute a new approach, or maybe even create a new strategic sourcing team. You won't realize this until you look at all the needs at once. It's likely patterns will emerge, and with that info, you can begin to order your work, develop priorities and launch an improvement plan.

You will want to set a final plan, with deadlines and accountabilities after sharing your initial strategy with business leaders, key hiring managers Be realistic, and do not bite off more than you can chew. What's important is that the business and the recruiters know that there is a plan, priorities have been set and that you can accomplish what you set out to do. Confirm with each constituency that you are focusing on the right priorities. And lastly, don't forget to get the stamp of approval from your boss, whether that is the head of TA, the head of HR or the recruiting director in your group.

As mentioned above, track and communicate your progress toward your goals. Make sure the recruiting teams feels ownership of the plan, thus giving them the responsibility of communicating wins (and losses). Talk about what has improved, the problems that have disappeared, and what they plan to tackle next. Watch as respect for the recruiting team grows.

Chapter 10 - Building a Great Recruiting Team

Finding a great recruiter is fairly easy. The job is pretty proscribed, so with a bit of training, almost anyone can do it. But finding a blend of someone who has the capacity to do recruiting well, to love it and finds its challenges interesting and far reaching enough to hold their attention for the long term is not as easy. Recruiting well can be nail-biting hard work. If it goes wrong, the recruiter gets blamed. If it goes well, the hiring manager gets the credit.

So if you're a recruiting leader, you're likely a glutton for punishment. Or perhaps you function well without a lot of praise or visibility. That's the nature of the game, baby! You're not in this for the glory. You're in it because you authentically want to win it!

The way you win, at large and small organizations, is to unleash the talents of (an always too small) recruiting team. The first thing you must learn to do as a recruiting leader is to select great recruiters for your team. I wish I could supply you with a formula but I'm afraid it's not that simple. As you become familiar with the orgs you work with, you will start to become familiar with the type of recruiting that's required to get the job done. For customer support, where the profiles don't change much, you need someone organized, fast and who is also a good selector of talent. For a deep technical org, you need a recruiter that is great at having conversations with hiring managers to understand the need, and who is great at helping managers and interviewers identify the skills and qualities necessary to get the job done. For leadership hiring, you might need a recruiter who can delicately help leaders discuss and agree on the profile as well as do a great job of selling the job to high-level candidates. Or your org might need to change the way it recruits. Maybe you need recruiters who can step up to the plate and help managers change the process, or open their minds to new types of candidates, or rely less on third-party recruiters. You will need to figure out what your org needs overall, and specifically what each sub org needs to select and evaluate recruiters. Remember the chapter about interviewing? It's important to understand what it is you're looking for before the process begins.

It's not very often that you walk into an organization that's a blank slate. Especially as a recruiting leader. You most likely are walking into a team that has grown organically. Perhaps they have seen leaders and managers come and go. In a new situation, your first job is to assess the team you have – what makes them successful, why their hiring teams love them. In some cases, you will meet with managers who are dissatisfied with the recruiting support they are receiving. You will have to figure out why the recruiter(s) have been unsuccessful, what complaints have been lodged, what do the client teams need? You will have to have deeper conversations and look at available data to determine if the recruiter needs additional skills, is overwhelmed or if it is matter of a changing talent market. Or perhaps the client team requires some change, or the overall process. Perhaps the group is lacking the appropriate tools. If you can, get them the tools that they need asap. Listen to their assessment of their situations, (especially the recruiters – all too often we tend to treat the complaints of hiring managers as gospel) and immediately set up time to meet with the org's managers and leaders to better understand what's working and what isn't working. Meet with the execs that run the group to find out the direction of the team, new products, services or methods, and take time to understand their perception of how well recruiting is going. Try not to make too many changes until you've done this work first. Write it up (see recruiting strategy summary above). More for your sake, than for others, but you may want to share with your leader as well, so that they understand how you are forming your opinions and they trust that you are looking deeply into the organization before presenting solutions.

Once you have a better idea of what's needed, you can begin to structure and select your team. It's not likely you will be able to start from scratch, but you will want to select the best of the talent available, assess who needs help and begin to prepare for who needs to go. Identify the kind of talent that you need to bring onto your team, stack rank the importance of each role, and begin to structure the teams based on the needs of the business. This is not easy to do, and you will, in most cases, do this quietly – that is, without the knowledge, at least in the beginning, of your recruiting team.

From my days at Recruiting Toolbox (and before that, even), I use a four-part method of looking at the roles and the talent on my team. Perhaps this might be helpful to you, too. Overall, as I assess team members, I am looking for their:

- **Skills** – what skills does the role require? Does the existing recruiter have these skills? If needed, can we augment their skills to ensure that they're able to meet the needs of the client team? Are they skilled enough at sourcing to get the job done? How skilled are they at interviewing and assessing candidates? Are they skilled at assessing compensation? Can they manage the paperwork and ATS data entry? Will they?

- **Qualities** – Do they have the competencies or qualities that make them a good fit for the organization? For example, if the company values direct, open communication, will they succeed? Another example -- the work might require a recruiter who can be analytical, who can parse data and draw and communicate conclusions. Are they the kind of recruiter who makes decisions rooted in analysis? If so, they will likely perform better than a recruiter who lives by instinct in this kind of company.

- **Achievements** – what has the recruiter done in the past to indicate that they would be able to handle similar work on my team? Have they proven they can deliver at a similar scope and scale? For example, do they have examples of creating effective strategies for handling demanding, high profile teams? If so, will their approach work well in your environment?

- **Motivation** – Does the recruiter want to be a recruiter? Are they motivated by the kind of work I will ask them to do? I am drawn to recruiters who want to be recruiters over those who want a way into HR. I think the qualities needed are inherently different. Are they interested in advancing in recruiting? Recruiting leadership?

Of course, you need to determine the skills, qualities, and achievements required for each role before I assess the candidates. And even though the title is the same, the role of "recruiter" might differ according to the needs of each group or team. For example, my tech recruiting team will likely require recruiters who are highly skilled at sourcing, who have made high-value tech hires in the past (achievements) and who love the work and love technology (motivation). It will be important for me to carefully think through the needs of each organization and to assess recruiters along these dimensions as I select and organize the teams.

I want to underscore my point here. Different groups require different types of recruiters. Some business units need sourcing experts. Others need recruiters who develop relationships and lead decisions. Some groups might need all these qualities and more. Your work as a leader is to identify the team needs, match recruiters to each group, and get training for the business groups as well as the recruiters to make it all work. It's not easy work, and as soon as you get one group settled, another need will develop. But that's why you're paid the big bucks!

Allow me to put on my trainer's hat for a moment. It's likely that both your recruiting team and your hiring managers could use some interview training. Often, when I would have initial discussions with clients, they would mention that they had developed training and all their managers had taken the training. When I would dig deeper, I'd learn that "training" consisted of an hour-long presentation and accompanying deck. That's a great start. But it's likely that your recruiters and hiring managers need more than a list of "do's and don'ts" and a quick guide on how to access candidates via the ATS. Do they know how to first determine their needs? Are they confident about their decisions? Are recruiters confident about the candidates they pass along? Are recruiters and hiring managers and interviewers good at assessing candidates, and expressing when candidates should be considered, or not considered? If you're not certain of the recruiting team and your hiring team's ability to interview well and select talent, then it's your responsibility as the recruiting leader to ensure that they get this training. Where to get this training? Again, excuse my bias, but you can find it here! (www.recruitingtoolbox.com)

Managing Your Recruiting Team

Building a great recruiting team was, perhaps, what I did best. I loved recognizing people who loved recruiting. People who went about the business of understanding the needs of their clients and delivering predictable, outstanding results.

What I learned, however, is that managing people isn't easy. You can manage your time, you can install a predictable format to capture what you learn about your people, you can set up a feedback review system to make sure people reviews get done on time. What you can't do is predict what problems and scenarios your people will face. What you can't predict is how you will need to intercede to help each person be successful.

So, here's how I do it. First, the recruiter or recruiting leader and I set a small list of goals to be accomplished each quarter. This list is typically a combination of what the recruiter/leader believes is needed to support the team, and the recruiter's own assessment of what he or she needs to improve, to move to the next level, or to satisfy professional goals.

Secondly, during every 1:1 (sometimes they were weekly, sometimes bi-weekly) I try to cover:

- How they are doing, personally and professionally? These are connected. A new parent worried about getting the baby to sleep might miss a deadline or an important deliverable. Sometimes a reminder is all that is needed. Sometimes, it means finding additional help or reducing the workload temporarily. It's better to have these conversations out loud and acknowledge that life sometimes gets in the way and a bit of problem-solving in advance can save our arses.

- Accomplishments. Did they get the offer signed? Wrap up all of their outstanding decline meetings? Get their entire team trained on the new ATS? It's important to acknowledge the work that gets accomplished. To take moment and bask in success. Reward when its warranted. Make sure you track this info so that you can refer to it during review time. I'm a big believer in quarterly – not annual -- reviews.

- What do they need to get over the hump this week? Could be a candidate hump, could be a hiring manager question, it might be project-related. Make sure that you elicit specific responses to this question. Make a note of the challenges. Volunteer to help or to find help if needed. If you're getting similar answers week after week, this might be an area where development or training is warranted.

- What do they plan to accomplish this week and this month? How are they tracking? Did they accomplish X last week? Shall we talk about last month's accomplishment?

Set quarterly review meetings to discuss the recruiter/leader's ongoing progress. If you have been conducting your 1:1's regularly, there shouldn't be any surprises here. Everything you talk about should have been covered during the 1:1 sessions. The quarterly review session should be spent talking about progress, new skills learned, paths to improvement and what's next from a career progression standpoint.

It's always my hope to remove the stress from these meetings. These meetings are only held to help the direct report get better, mark progress and take on new assignments when they are ready. Recruiting is one of those professions where in the moment coaching (or directly after) works best. Storing up accusations and waiting to spring them on your direct report is no way to elicit their best performance. Make feedback a regular part of communication, and always make time to be sure the feedback has been understood (and that I understood the situation well) and a way of improving performance, not stifling performance.

When managing recruiters, I found that the primary issues included right-sizing the number of reqs they carried, and getting them to improve on that, and the ability to engage with hiring managers and communicate effectively.

Of course, I had to learn all of this, person by person, and got better over time. I think my true desire to see "my" recruiters and recruiting managers as successful helped to drive so many to take on bigger, important roles at all kinds of companies. I'm lucky to call many of these colleagues' friends, and never hesitate to call on them for feedback and advice!

Chapter 11 – Operations: Recruiting Metrics: You'll Always Need Data

Are you recruiting the right employees as fast as you can? That's what every hiring manager wants to know, in a nutshell. "Right" employee is subjective. And any measurement of "right" will occur so long in the past that it becomes meaningless. "As fast as you can" is dependent on several factors. The talent market, for one. Is speed really what's needed? No, really? Why so fast? Does recruiting for speed prevent you from hiring the quality you need? Are you so focused on doing it so quickly that you fail to do it well, or fail to plan for future needs? Do you hire candidates that decide to leave within a year or two? Are you frustrated because you can't pay the top salaries that your talent competitors pay? Then perhaps your strategy of hiring quickly is failing you.

But answering this question – are you recruiting the right employees as fast as you can – is perhaps the most difficult task asked of recruiting. We don't shoulder all the responsibility for selecting the "right" employee, nor do we own what happens to the employee once they arrive (we might have selected the right employee, but once they arrive, business conditions, or leadership style, or any other number of factors might have changed.) So we settle for reporting what we do control:

- Time to fill
- Hires made by department, hiring manager, or recruiter

- Cost (salary) to fill
- Time to accept and to start

I believe that only metrics that represent the opportunity to improve results should be presented. There are numbers that help our businesses. Number of projected starts. Backfill vs. new hires. Hires by group or division, and trending data associated with each group. Your first job is to understand what reports are out there, and how useful they are. What do managers actually use? And how are these numbers useful? What decisions are made based on these numbers? Collect this information from every business unit you support, as well as other orgs (such as Finance) who use the reporting to understand what has happened or to project what will happen in the future. Figure out how you can deliver 90% of this via one consolidated, easy-to-read report, every week (the report should be adjustable so that each business unit is presented with information relevant to that group). The other 10% might not require weekly reporting or may not even be important to the majority of your stakeholders.

Then get to work on a set of metrics that help you, the head of talent for your division or company, become more successful. You will need to look at recruiter behavior, overall org results, external talent market projections and anything else that will help you prepare for what's next. Divide your reporting into three time frames; what's happened in the past, what's happening right now (this quarter) and projected numbers. Each have their distinct uses throughout the org. And, what you report from the past should inform your projections.

I suggest that you never release a report that doesn't measure over time (or compare time periods) the effectiveness of whatever it is you are reporting on. A leader typically doesn't have the time to root through your data to figure out what's working and what's not. Share a few bar charts or graphs to help them quickly understand if hires are increasing or decreasing and add a few bullet points to explain why. That kind of report is useful. A report full of lines of names of new hires with no assessment of impact, or quantity, or quality or relationship is useless!

I would argue that understanding Talent Availability is likely one of the first things you can do to help your orgs recruit faster, from the right sources. This data is typically a little harder, or more expensive to collect, and rarely is it 100% correct. What you are looking for here is directional guidance. At what rate are students graduating from computer science programs? How does that compare to projected hiring in your industry? How in demand are financial analysts, and how is compensation changing? From there it is your job to make informed guesses about what these numbers mean for your organization.

Once you have figured out what is important to your leaders (and what is important to you), send a monthly or quarterly report to your leader and their direct reports. You will want to make this easy to digest. Pose and answer 1-2 high-level, answerable questions. Add to this list as leaders consume the data and ask additional questions. Be thoughtful about what you include and don't include in this report, consider the behavioral changes or conversations you'd like to initiate based on the data.

Adopt a look for your recruiting metrics, perhaps an identifiable logo, and don't send any reports without this branding. Make your reports must-read for your leaders.

Additionally, your org will likely ask recruiting to contribute to monthly or quarterly reports by business units or the exec team. Find out what the requirements are in advance and have these ready at the appointed time each month. Get to know the folks in finance who put these reports together – they can be fantastic resources when it comes to reporting information in a way that the executive team can easily digest.

Lastly, release reports on a regular cadence, and make them readily available on Slack or other central storage accessible to managers and leadership.

Chapter 12 – Operations: Structure, Process and Tools

We have talked a bit about team structure, but you will want to double down here and keep a close eye on how you've organized the team (or how it has been organized in the past by a different leader). Depending on the size and needs of your team, leadership positions on your team, tools, and other factors, you might decide to centralize or decentralize the recruiting organization or for my money, build a combo loosely decentralized, centralized team.

Recruiting teams, depending on the orgs they serve, operate differently. They require different sourcing methods, different interviewing structures, different decision-making processes. The success metrics will look different, and each team will operate optimally using a different set of tools.

That said, the organization – and you, the leader – likely require a common way of looking at the landscape of TA. The metrics that indicate success may differ, but the way that you see and review those metrics should be the same. To put it another way, your tech recruiting team may find that five hires per recruiter per month is an optimal, desired metric. Your customer service recruiting team may find that five times as many – 25 hires per month per recruiter – is optimal. But both teams should be using the same tools, the same methodology to track and report out their numbers.

You, and hiring managers, should be able to access this information from a tool that works from anywhere. Similarly, each divisional recruiting team will likely require supporting tools, recruitment marketing support, reporting and administrative support. Centralizing these efforts makes sense and ensures that you will be able to deliver these basic services on a more efficient, and cost-efficient, basis.

You will also want to ensure that your recruiting team continuously optimizes and upgrades skills – an important key to retaining top recruiters.

So let me take a stab at illustrating what decentralized/centralized recruiting might look like:

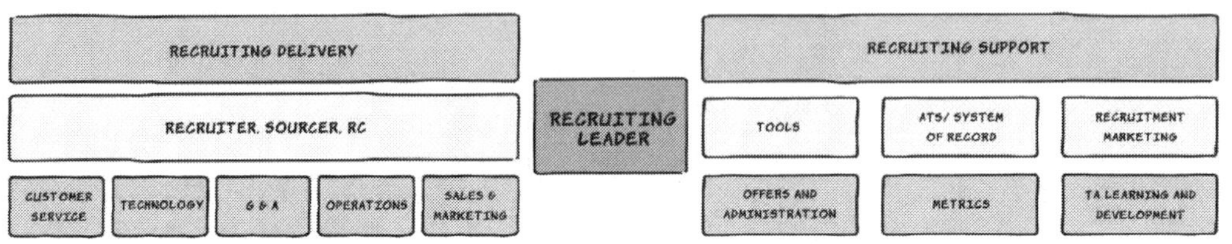

[Illustration 12]

As you can see, in my dreamworld, recruiting delivery is more closely related to the business it supports, led by a recruiting leader or recruiter who has close ties to leadership in the business. I wouldn't go so far as to have that recruiting leader report to the business (a truly decentralized model), but I would make sure that the recruiting leader and the business leader were closely connected. In larger organizations, each senior business leader should be connected to a recruiting manager or director able to track and solve the recruiting challenges, understands the corresponding talent market, tools, methods, and metrics, and who can help the leader think through the kinds of talent that will augment the existing team. That is the kind of talent advising our businesses need, and that is how we grow and flourish, share our knowledge and exert appropriate influence to deserve the title of talent advisor.

Once you have identified the structure that works best in your organization, and you have a good idea of what your team needs, it's time to work on the process. It's likely that a process already exists – has existed for some time – and you may find quite a bit of resistance to change. Or, the org wants change, but everyone seems to have an opinion about what change looks like. The truth is it is unlikely a group of business leaders and managers know exactly what change is needed. They have great ideas, of course, but they are unable to see the entire recruiting org and process from more than their own perspective. It is important, after conversations with leaders, managers and recruiters to sketch out a plan, and get confirmation from key players in each group that your plan is the right plan. And I would break the plan into quarters. You will be lucky to have a year in your job to execute your plan, at the current rate of change. So, break up your plan into four parts, achievable in a year. If you are lucky enough to have another year in your TA leadership role, then by all means, go for year two. But let's start with successfully implementing a 1-year plan to get your org running smoothly.

Let's say your plan looks something like this:

	GOAL	Q1	Q2	Q3	Q4
SOURCING	• ENSURE SOURCERS HAVE THE SKILLS NEEDED TO FIND GREAT CANDIDATES • GREATLY REDUCE THE USE OF EXTERNAL RECRUITERS	REVIEW AND SELECT SOURCING TRAINING OPTIONS	PILOT AND TRACK SOURCING TRAINING SUCCESS; ADJUST AS NEEDED	• ROLL OUT TRAINING BROADLY • ADJUST RULES OF ENGAGEMENT FOR AGENCIES	• REVIEW AND ADJUST SOURCING SUCCESS • ADDITIONAL SOURCING TRAINING AS NEEDED
ASSESMENT	• TRAIN HIRING MANAGERS • ENSURE RECRUITERS SUPPORT TRAINING	COLLECT FEEDBACK ABOUT EVERYTHING	• PILOT INTERVIEW TRAINING • DELIVER TRAINING TO RECRUITING TEAM	BEGIN TRAINING ROLLOUT	• REVIEW RESULTS OF ROLLOUT • CONTINUE ROLLOUT
TOOLS AND DATA	EVALUATE NEEDS AND SELECT NEW ATS	EVALUATE TOOLS	SELECT SYSTEM, COMPLETE CONTRACT	• ROLL OUT PILOT, TEST • GATHER AND ADDRESS FEEDBACK	BEGIN PHASED ROLLOUT OF NEW SOLUTION

[Illustration 13]

This will be your guiding document for the next year. You must first socialize your plan with each constituency, ensuring that each group understands the "why" of the plan, and ensuring that each group enthusiastically buys off on the plan. I suggest reviewing this with each constituency in monthly updates, keeping yourself honest and keeping your teams updated. On a quarterly basis I'd do a live update, making sure to highlight successes (and successful team members) and making sure to motivate where needed. Remember, this lives with the leadership team, each hiring manager and each recruiter. Include all these groups in regular updates.

One of the most important things you must do as a recruiting leader is track requisitions. Until you get this right, you will have no peace. Ensure that there is one system of record (usually a feature of or integrated with your ATS) and do what you must do to make sure that it is 100% accurate at all times. It may take a longer time than expected to get to 100%, but it's worth it to be the dependable source of truth when it comes to understanding the number of open positions, the number of filled positions, the number of budgeted positions, etc. If, for any reason, there are two sources of req data, you're screwed. The numbers will never match and will always be questioned. Other requisition considerations:

- Approval process – who is required, what information is required, who grants the final approval

- Overall open positions, by manager, rolled up to leadership

- Overall approved positions, filled and unfilled, new vs. backfill, open vs. not yet open vs. closed (or filled)

- Historical backfill by business unit, with a comparison to prior year(s) to track engagement

- Annual list of approved new positions, by business unit, compared YOY

This information will be treasured by finance teams, leaders and managers. It will come in handy during the "pull back" season – when execs, unsure of whether the company will hit its financial targets, will want to hold off, slow down or completely cut off recruiting for new positions. It's better to have this information always on hand, already trusted, than trying to scramble to pull it together when it's needed. In fact, it's a great idea to keep your eye on this information, noting when hiring gets too frothy.

Another practice I've observed is the ranking of open positions – a simple A, B or C scale, where managers or leaders rank the order in which positions should be opened and hired. That way, if the dreaded pull back season happens, you will have recruited for the most important positions first, leaving the less critical positions until you're able to recruit again. This also puts the weight of determining what's most important on the business and business leader. You as the recruiter or recruiting leader do not want to be in the business of determining what's most important.

This reminds of a story from my time at Amazon. I was excited that my team had filled most of the open roles in record time. I shared the data with the CTO, who told me, "That's great. But I would trade having hired for this position (he pointed to an open, hard to fill position on my list) over all of those. That's how critical that job is to the business." I left his office a little deflated, but so much smarter than before. From that point I never forgot the important lesson that jobs are not equally important.

I also want to mention tracking traffic patterns – where talent is coming from, and where it is going. It might be a bit difficult to pull this together each month or each quarter, but definitely worth it. Look at your sourcing data first, to figure out where talent is coming from and if that has changed recently. You will want to track this data over time, for different, critical job titles, and you will want to look at speed and source of hire. Who is coming in, from what companies? How fast are you hiring them? Are they coming from referrals? How does compensation fit in the picture? Pick three or four companies, engage your sourcing team to do a deep dive into why you're seeing so much talent move from these companies to yours, interview recent hires and share the pros and cons of hiring from these companies. Publish a report every quarter to keep your recruiters and hiring managers educated. Conversely, work with HR to get exit data and develop a similar report about your important talent competitors – where are people going and why, and share that data as well. This kind of info helps your recruiters and hiring managers become aware of talent market challenges and perhaps address issues before they become problems!

Lastly, as recruiting leaders, we have to ensure our organizations are getting smarter – better, faster – over each quarter. This naturally happens over time, for some. I'm a big believer in short bites of learning, though I made a living delivering big training programs to organizations hungry for it. My advice to clients who wanted our interview training or talent advisor training was to plan for what would happen after the training. How would you keep the learning alive? How would you make sure that knowledge trickled down from leader to team member to new hire?

As TA leader, sponsor a monthly or quarterly learning lab for the TA team. Attendance mandatory. Then invite internal or external guests who help us get smart about the talent market, or assessment methods, or market compensation or our new ATS, or anything else your team tells you they'd like to improve. We don't do this enough in TA. Our worlds are constantly changing, new tools appear in the marketplace, candidates start to act differently. Let's stay sharp!

Additionally, it's important to help the larger org get smart about talent. I talked about circulating a quarterly report, but make sure you embed TA training into your company's fabric. Not just how to use the ATS and where to find the forms, but share deep knowledge on interviewing and selection, the talent market, how to negotiate compensation etc. Offer this programming quarterly on a first-come, first-served basis, and watch the sessions "sell" out! Invite outsiders to provide perspective (book authors, speakers, recruiting leaders in town for a conference) and insiders to provide guidance (how a recruiting team enhanced their college recruiting program). Make sure the content is at the right level, and you will have managers and leaders knocking down doors to save their spot. I had my first taste of this at Amazon, where we would invite a famous author to speak (we had an advantage here, but often a small investment can net you just the author you'd want to address your audience). When a talent-related speaker would come to speak, there would be standing room only. I still have my signed copy of *Love 'Em* or *Lose 'Em* co-authored by Beverly Kay, a book that keeps retention top of mind and encouraged many of the managers at Amazon to think more deeply about retaining the talent on their teams. These days, we can just as easily share provocative articles, podcasts and videos and, as talent advisors, this is exactly what we should be doing.

Chapter 13 – Operations: Employee Referral Programs

One of the most important processes for any recruiting team is the Employee Referral Program (I'll shorten to ERP going forward). It's likely your ERP accounts for a third or more of your hires. ERPs are, with perhaps one exception, the best source of candidates. (Without intentional effort, ERPs might negatively impact the diversity of candidates, but we will talk about a way to achieve greater diversity through ERPs shortly.)

I talked briefly about my experience at Yahoo! launching a needed ER program. As part of a big promotion, the TA team initiated efforts to attract applicants through a variety of methods, the ER program offered the most, and the most consistent, results. The most important lessons I learned in launching the ER program:

- Make sure your referral system works. Test it. Refer a couple of folks and see what happens. The first thing I learned at Yahoo! was that the referral system technology was broken and had been for months. (We roped in a couple of developers to quickly fix it!)

- Referral bonuses matter, but not as much as the social clout of being able to get a great job for a friend. Treat every referral as valuable, and work hard to find the right place for the referral (don't leave that work for the employee – often employees aren't as aware of talent pathways as the recruiting team).

Respond – quickly – to every referral and update the referring employee as well.

- Referral bonus systems are buttressed by a bunch of rules and regulations. Make sure that you dot your i's. Some things to consider:
  - Eligibility. Who can participate, and who is ineligible (recruiting? HR? Leaders? Managers? Managers referring someone to their own team? Ethics play a big role here, and should be considered, written down and signed off)
  - Referral bonus amounts and rewards. Keep tax considerations in mind. Remember that prizes, such as trips or technology or even vehicles are subject to taxation.
  - Referral eligibility. Consider the length of time an employee is eligible to receive a bonus for referring a candidate. Make sure your system time stamps receipt of a referral, and checks for prior submittals. If referrals expire, make sure your system handles that automatically, and sends an update to the referring employee. And, make sure you think through Agency candidates vs. referral candidates, making sure the correct party gets consideration.
  - Fraud. If you work for an organization of some size, you will likely be challenged by someone attempting to game the system. Figure out a way to stop this before it happens. I once found an employee in a remote office advertising open positions, having emails sent to her, and then submitting those candidates as referrals!

One of the most critical actions you can take is to continuously market your referral program, keeping an eye on the number of submittals and the percentage of referral hires. Remember, your marketing plan must include marketing to employees about the program, and sharing the results (bonuses paid, newly referred employees, etc.). In addition, share program results with the recruiting team and leadership to encourage further investment and support.

You will want to measure and compare YOY results of your referral plan, by tracking

- % of employees participating (measures morale & engagement)
- Yield (the number of referred candidates that get hired, and as compared to other sources)
- +/- referral hires
- +/- referrals
- +/- unique referrers
- Diversity of referral hires
- Time to disposition referred candidates

You will also want to consider diversity as you build out your referral program. The first thing I'd do is map out the diversity of referred candidates. How many women get referred? How many are hired from this group? Are there areas, like tech, where women are under- represented (as compared to all referrals, as well as compared to the overall talent market). Do the same with all other under-represented groups. Discuss your findings with your diversity advisors (smaller orgs may not have them) and talk about ways to increase diverse referrals.

The one thing you and the recruiting team can do is discuss a plan of action with your hiring managers. Looking at the overall diversity of the team and figuring out how to change its composition by encouraging employees to refer more diverse candidates. I think this works better if recruiters talk with HR and managers 1:1, as needed, to address the why and how to diversify the team, and to figure out how to tap into existing networks to extract referrals. Often, this is a matter of talking with team leaders about the need for diversity (this often requires more discussion than is obvious) and extracting targeted referrals. A team in search of additional women leaders, for example, should talk about the need, and remind referrers that they needn't know the person well. Knowledge about the candidate's reputation is enough to get the ball rolling. The recruiting team will reach out to the referred candidate, and every candidate will go through the recruiting process, so referrers needn't fear candidates slipping through without being thoroughly interviewed and assessed. (I could make note of how women or minority candidates are often suspected of doing just this – slipping through the cracks – though history and the numbers tell us that it is more often white male candidates referred by other white male candidates who are likely to "slip through." My recommendation is that no one is allowed to get through the process without submitting to a thorough interview process.)

If your organization has well established diversity resource groups, or employee resource groups (ERGs), it is a good idea to partner with each group to extract referrals. Simple reminders are helpful, but assigning a recruiter to each group can help facilitate the process and likely elicit more, and more diverse, referrals.

When it comes to referrals, it is worth it to implement a solid marketing plan. To ensure the referral system is a constant source of high-quality candidates, you will have to remind employees of its existence and continuously make employee referrals attractive. Use the company intranet, Slack channels, posters in the elevator, and any other method acceptable in your org to remind employees of their opportunity to bring great talent into the company (and earn substantial referral bonuses). Make it easy for recruiters and hiring managers to promote the program within their org and every once in a while, when there is a great need, increase the referral bonus for all positions or a subset of positions.

Keep an eye on your metrics to ensure the breadth of employees who refer job candidates is great – you do not want a small subset of people referring candidates. You want everyone to feel as if they can help the company build a high performing team by referring candidates from their professional (or other) networks.

Lastly, make sure you acknowledge referrers and referral hires every chance you get. I've worked on referral promotions where we created posters of the employee and the new hire/referred candidate. The posters were quite popular, if you measure by the number of posters that mysteriously ended up decorating desk areas (lesson learned: print a few extra).

Chapter 14 – Operations: Internal Hiring

Managing referrals well is important but it is more important, I think, to manage internal movement in your organization. Typically, a significant portion of hires can be attributed to internal movement, and many HR leaders will sing the praises of hiring internal candidates: More satisfied employees, less time/money spent on recruiting, seamless integration requiring less onboarding, employees that stay longer, fewer team upsets, to name a few.

I've seen several different models of managing internal recruiting, each with its own set of flaws:

Internal apply/compete – where internal candidates view/apply open positions in the org, applies (usually through the same portal as external candidates.) This works well, until it doesn't. This method becomes challenging if scores of unqualified internal candidates apply. Or if the existing manager isn't prepared for team members to leave for a different team. Or if candidate assessment is viewed as unfair.

HR-identified candidates – where HR has designated certain roles/candidates to support internal growth, or to accommodate the acquisition of new skills. To do this well, HR, Recruiting and the management team must work seamlessly to plan for and accommodate these employee promotions and job changes. The most common problem here is unfair, or uneven promotion of some employees over others. Reminder: Doing this well includes buttoned up, transparent communication in all directions.

Promotions/movement within the team – I've seen this happen with only the slightest involvement from the recruiting team, leaving hiring managers and candidates confused. When conducted together, promotions that involve both HR and recruiting, as well as the hiring manager have the best chance of smooth navigation within the organization and promoting the best person for the job. When recruiting is involved in these discussions, there is a greater chance of understanding the skills and qualities needed to do the job, a greater understanding of the value that an internal candidate might bring over an external candidate, as well as a greater understanding of what skills the internal candidate might lack (and thus perhaps inform the HR team of necessary training). Recruiting can bring a view of the external talent market (how expensive is the talent, does it exist in sufficient quantity, would external talent bring something to the team that doesn't currently exist, etc.). HR can bring a view of internal mechanisms that might better inform recruiting and the hiring manager (potential org changes, promotion readiness, etc.)

If not conducted in strong partnership with HR, internal recruiting can get messy!

Make sure your employees understand how internal movement works at your company. Especially if internal talent will compete with external talent:

- Monthly or quarterly updates on internal movement to managers and employees via internal email, slack or intranet

- Visible reminders that help employees know what positions are open and how to apply

- Shout outs and celebration of employee promotions and changes

- Frequent 'how to' reminders – rules of the road, how to apply for a new position, when promotions or moves are typically approved, the process – reminders that internal candidates often compete with external candidates

- Keep in mind that the process should be transparent – easy to navigate. Remind employees that internal movement is the best source of candidates for the company!

Interviewing internal candidates places additional responsibilities in the lap of hiring managers. They must be extra careful about the job skills and qualities, so that internal candidates know what's expected. Hiring managers should be able to easily articulate why an internal (or any) candidate did or did not get the job. For rejected internal candidates, hiring managers should be willing to spend some time with the candidate explaining the rejection, and the steps required to be successful the next time around.

Work with your HR partners to better understand career pathing for the roles where promotion is most likely and spend some time and effort explaining these steps to your cadre of internal candidates.

Make sure that the manager provides direct feedback to the candidate and the candidate's manager. The feedback should be constructive with actionable steps the employee can take to qualify for the position at a later time.

Chapter 15 – Operations: Tools, Tools, Tools

Recruiting, good recruiting, requires more than an ATS system. From sourcing tools to recruitment marketing solutions to interviewing and assessment platforms, there is always a new tool promising to make recruiting better, easier, faster.

Here's the problem. There are far too many tools to know about or evaluate all of them (so far, we've indexed over 2400 tools helpful to recruiters on recruiterhunt.com). Secondly, claims about making recruiters faster are dubious, at best. So far, nothing much has changed the average days to fill for most positions since the 1990s, when I got into this business. Not to say that recruiting hasn't improved since Toni Braxton first belted out "Unbreak My Heart" (1996). But hiring a project manager then takes about the same amount of time that it takes now.

As someone who looks at a significant number of tools each month, my advice is to spend a little time, and eventually a little money, trying a few of these tools each quarter. Listen to the recruiting team, ask them what problems they're experiencing, and figure out if there is a tool that might help. Try a few sourcing tools but look for other type of tools that might help your team schedule faster, interview better, close with more confidence. There are AI tools that can help you write outreach email. Any part of the process that can be automated, someone is out there, building a tool. Before you implement any tool, you'll have to assess your appetite and readiness:

- Can we afford it? How expensive will the tool be, from onboarding, training to ongoing integration? Does this tool fit into my budget indefinitely?

- What is the longevity of a tool like this?
- Does this functionality already exist in our ATS or other tools? How expensive would it be to turn it on? Does the tool already integrate with our current ATS?
- Will the tool be used by team, consistently? Is it easy to learn? Are there live and documented training options? What happens when new people join our team?
- How does using the tool create additional value to the recruiting process? To hiring managers and leaders? For how long do you estimate this tool will provide value, and under what circumstances does it stop delivering value?
- Who else is using this tool? What do they have to say about it? What has it improved? Is it a worthwhile investment?
- How will we choose from the different vendors? What features are absolutely must have, and which are optional? How will price figure in our decision?

You may want to select a small subcommittee to help you evaluate and select recruiting tools. At the very least you will want to evaluate and confirm that each new tool does what it says it does, that the functionality supports your recruiting function, that it integrates with existing tools and methods, especially your ATS, that users find it easy and intuitive and use it appropriately and frequently enough to ensure that the cost is justified, that the tool has adequate support and training, and that your recruiting org can afford it.

When possible, work with the sales rep (or the creator of the tool, if it is new enough in the market) to establish a trial run of the product in your environment. Share your criteria for success with the sales rep in advance. Often, you will find that features promised are non-existent. If the feature is critical for success with the tool, then extend your trial until the feature is a reality. If you're early, you may be lucky enough to be part of an extended trial period in exchange for your feedback. Take this responsibility seriously. Be forthright and you will find that vendors value your feedback, and you will be asked to evaluate new technology regularly. Don't overextend your evaluation period in the interest of getting access to a new tool that you plan to abandon. Vendors can see you coming, and karma is a bitch! If you must, negotiate a short-term or reduced-access deal in the interest of using the tool while you lobby for the budget to pay for the tool.

In any case, keep a clear record of the tools you pay for, when they're up for renewal. Review the monthly usage reports (insist on these, or you might find yourself paying for a whole host of well thought-of but completely unused tools). Talk to your team before you start renewal negotiations. In fact, talk to your peers at other companies that use the tool. The more knowledge you're willing to share, the more you can collect to use during negotiations. Keep in mind, the goal isn't to get the cheapest price possible, it's to get the best tool to help your team achieve the results needed at the best price. Work with your rep to achieve that.

Don't forget to create a budget – for both your team and your tools – and revisit often. Keep track of estimated and actual costs, and review the budget before negotiating on any tool, any salary, and before reporting on or changing any budget allocation.

Chapter 16 - What's Your Employer Brand?

I talked a bunch about my experience at Yahoo when we embarked on a journey to understand and better communicate our employer brand. It was imperative that we posed and attempted to answer the question of who we were as an employer and what it meant when candidates joined the company. With so much at stake, and being in such a visible position, we had to get it right. And I think, for the time, we did. You are likely in a more fortunate position and have a bit more latitude to discover who you are, and who you want to be, and how you will use this knowledge to attract top candidates. To reiterate, you'll need to answer a few questions before you're able to determine your employer brand, and you'll need to pose these questions to every around to deeply understand your organization:

- Externally, how does the world view your organization? Think locally and globally. What are the good and the bad things potential candidates understand (or even misunderstand) about your culture? What do they believe about your executives? About your financial position? About your products or services? About how you rank among your competitors? Your talent competitors?

- Similarly, consider your candidate experience. Where do you rank among your talent competitors? What characteristics – real or imagined – do interviewers ascribe to your organization? What do candidates read about your org on Glassdoor or similar sites?

- Internally, how do your people feel about working for your organization? What makes them proud? What do they talk about to their friends? What makes them refer (or not refer) candidates? What would they like to see improved? What do they view as wasteful or not worth the effort when it comes to attracting candidates?

There are likely a hundred more questions that could be asked, the idea here is to open a dialogue and gather enough feedback to begin to shape a picture. Ideally, gathering this data would involve both a survey (where participants are anonymous) and smaller focus groups. You will want to have the survey feedback as the genesis of the focus groups, and you will want to have groups of senior execs, groups of employees from every part of the company, and groups of all levels. The idea is to put together a statement that speaks openly of who you are as an organization – what's most important in terms of what you do, and what behaviors are most important to get it done. And it's OK if this statement is big and aspirational. It should reflect the best of who you are and who you want to be.

FYI, I am no expert in employer branding. Everything I know came from employer branding experts with whom I've had the pleasure of working or some home-grown knowledge I've spun up. (Remember that temp job I wrote about earlier. The one where they had me sit in the lobby? Well, soon after that I got a job in advertising, where my interest in how humans respond to messaging never waned. Shout out to Davis Harrison Dion Advertising in Chicago!) All this to say, that if you can afford it, get some help with this important, foundational work. Getting this right can be the difference in attracting – and being attractive to – top candidates or middling candidates. Do this well, and you will be able to attract just the candidates whom you want – those who will do well in your environment.

It's also important to deeply understand how you're viewed externally by candidates and potential candidates. Review all of the interview feedback surveys available to you and read the feedback written by employees and candidates on Glassdoor, Indeed, Levels.fyi, Comparably and more. Take this feedback with a grain of salt – the feedback is much more likely to come from rejected candidates so don't worry about a harsh review. If the same type of comment shows up regularly, however, it's a good idea to listen to what's said. If lots of candidates say that interviewers ask easy questions, and don't particularly pay attention to the answers, they may be right, and you likely have a problem to solve within your community of interviewers.

With a deeper understanding of who you are, and what you want, and how you're viewed, you can craft an employer brand that speaks to what you have to offer, who thrives in your environment in a realistic, albeit slightly aspirational, way.

While your employee value proposition speaks plainly about the type of employee that thrives in your environment, your employer brand should be a bit razzle-dazzle, attracting desirable employees that are attracted to your brand, your products and services, your employees and managers and your way of working. Again, unless you have the creative chops to craft just the right messaging, or if you're working with a minimal budget, it might be helpful to get help here. I think working with the marketing team at Yahoo helped us clarify and define the problems we needed to solve, the questions we needed to answer (for employees as well as prospective candidates) and the messaging that would work. We opted to work with our internal marketing team not because we couldn't afford to work with an agency, but because our internal marketing team really understood our urgency and our dilemma. But I've worked with advertising agencies that focused on employer branding who delivered excellent work. Whether the recruiting team, the marketing team or an external agency provides the employer brand, you will want to check in with your internal marketing team to ensure that your employer brand complements your overall brand and that your roll-out and delivery doesn't interfere with any overall corporate or product branding efforts.

As you think about messaging, it might help to create a candidate persona grid (two or three should do, resist the urge to create something for every team. Focus on those roles that are hardest to recruit, where there is quite a bit of recruiting activity, where you would expect external messaging to influence potential candidates)

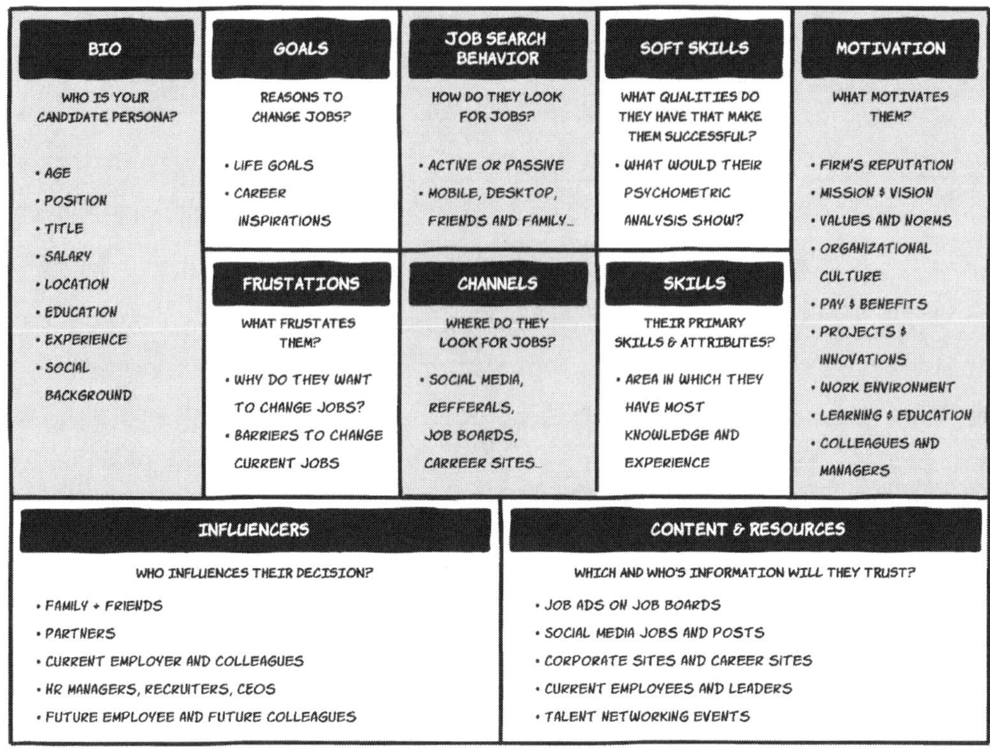

[Illustration 14]

Once you have nailed the messaging, create a marketing strategy that helps you achieve the desired results. You may want to change an existing opinion about your org. Or, like Yahoo, you may have an urgent need to stand out against your talent competitors. Or perhaps your need is not so urgent, you are a new entrant into the talent marketplace, and you want to make sure that great talent considers your organization alongside others in your space. Understanding the outcomes you want to achieve will help you narrow your set of activities and begin to measure what campaign activities work.

A reminder – don't forget to test your messaging with existing employees. From them, you'll get an honest opinion of your branding attempts. They will let you know if they feel comfortable sharing your messaging with their friends, if it rings true, if your humor is truly funny or if you're trying too hard. I can't tell you the number of messaging mistakes we would have made had we not conducted focus groups with different collections of employees.

Lastly, measure what you can measure. We were lucky enough to be able to capture quite a bit about our employee referral program. We could take a look at applications and draw conclusions about how certain activities impacted candidate flow. But there were some activities, such as television or billboards (we didn't incorporate QR-code technology) that were hard to pin down. I'm sure they had some effect on attracting candidates, I just can't tell you with any certainty that they were worth the investment. I remember arguing against some of approaches, certain they would be a waste of money, but the engineering team was keen to try all sorts of things. And because we were fighting for more than candidates, publicity was high on the list of end goals. And, boy did we get publicity! But in the end, we knew, without a doubt, that our efforts increased applications, increased referrals and increased hires.

Chapter 17 – Troubleshooting: The Job of the Recruiting Leader

Perhaps you've made it to management, and you're floundering a bit when it comes to understanding your purpose. Happens to the best of us. I can tell you how I viewed my job. At the manager level, I was a troubleshooter. I worked closely with recruiters to help them resolve whatever issue stood in the way of making hires. Often, my role was as a sounding board for the recruiters on my team – giving them the space to talk about challenges out loud and working with them to come up with solutions. When I think back about the work I've done, I might have enjoyed sourcing immensely, but I get the most satisfaction when I think of how the recruiters on my team, after just a bit of encouragement or creative brainstorming, stepped up and got the job done. Occasionally, it was imperative that I work with hiring teams to figure out a larger issue, or work through some impenetrable problem to create a better environment for recruiting. (Example: when there was a disparity in our company's comp, our talent competitor's comp and being able to pay what we needed to pay to get the talent we wanted, it was my job to step in, do the upfront surveying work, talk with the hiring manager, the comp team, and others to make the changes necessary, or to help develop a sourcing strategy or communication approach to get the talent we needed). I tried to never embark on this kind of a journey alone, getting a talented recruiter involved and preparing them for next step toward leadership.

At higher levels of leadership, I viewed my role as less involved with day-to-day tactics of my team (although you cannot be too far removed -- recruiting is a full contact sport), and put more thought into overall recruiting team effectiveness: Do we, as an organization, have a great handle on who/how many we need to recruit? Are we focused on what the future will require? Do we have a recruiting team that can deliver our current and future needs? Could we deliver all that we said we could deliver? Did we need additional resources or tools to get the job done? Are we moving fast enough to get the right talent in the door? Does our compensation model meet the market and afford us the kind of talent we need?

It's likely that for every leadership role, the set of problems to be solved varies greatly. My best advice: don't take on too much. It's tempting, especially, if you think you have the answers. But at the outset, commit to deeply understanding the problems, from all viewpoints – recruiter, hiring manager, leadership and candidate – and understanding the overall environment so that you can rank the importance of each problem set. Armed with the knowledge, set your plan and get to work. You will want to revisit your plan regularly, to make sure that you are delivering results, in the time that you committed, and to check that you're working on the right problems. In a modern organization, the talent needs can change on a dime – always keep that in mind.

From my experience, recruiting challenges can be bucketed in a few groups;

Recruiter Performance – recruiters sometimes do a poor job of communicating with hiring managers, affecting their ability to source quickly, interview effectively or help recruiting teams make decisions. Some of this can and should be addressed by ongoing training. Some of this can be improved through consistent ongoing coaching and leadership.

Sometimes it might be necessary to take a look at recruiter workload (or req load). This is tough because depending on the position, the market, the hiring manager and a dozen other factors, workloads vary. The way to help recruiters manage workloads is to measure their performance. Take an initial guess by looking at what the recruiter for the particular business unit has done in the past. Mark that as the baseline. At the end of the quarter, review the req load and determine if it is appropriate or if it needs adjustment. Perhaps add a stretch goal. After a few quarters, you'll have a better idea of what's possible, and what's to be expected, and what needs to change to improve the numbers. Have an open discussion with each recruiter about their numbers during each quarterly review. And keep in mind that req loads can fluctuate because of market conditions – candidates that were once plentiful might dry up and vice versa.

Hiring Manager Performance – hiring managers are often unaware of their vital role in the recruiting process and do not or cannot make the efforts needed to confidently lead to outstanding hires. Again, training works here, but you must be able to deliver training on a regular basis, as leadership/hiring managers change frequently. It's also important to find out the leaders in your org who support recruiting and deeply understand its importance. Give these leaders everything they need to continuously message the importance of recruiting well. Pair them with effective recruiter/recruiting leader to deliver these messages consistently and use this group as an example to others.

Process – recruiting efforts that lack a standard process lead to greater inefficiency all around, as well as the ability to measure and change performance. An example would be recruiting kickoff – without an understood, measured method of kicking off every position, the practice is ineffective and happens infrequently. Make sure managers know what they can expect, and what they are expected to contribute. How should recruiters conduct the kickoff process and within what time frame? What is the expected output of kickoff meetings? Putting some reins around the process, what it should look like, and how effectiveness will be measured will help everyone involved in recruiting.

Tools – Having the right tools to manage the process is imperative, especially if your recruiting team has grown to some size, or you're hiring an awful lot of people. Beyond your ATS, what do your recruiters need to be effective? What do your recruiting coordinators need? Your hiring managers? Your candidates? Having a good grip on this and being ready to pull the trigger when you get the budget makes all the difference. You will also likely need some help evaluating tools, and if you don't have a person or team dedicated to this, you may want to find a few folks on your team that can help. I have found that sourcers are often great at this and have a deep interest in helping to select the tools that make your org hum. Figure out how you will evaluate and prioritize testing and set aside time to have deep discussions on how your tools are serving the process and the stakeholders.

Chapter 18 – Recruiting and Legal Requirements

As a recruiting leader, as a recruiter, even, you have a responsibility to uphold legal regulations applied to the recruiting process. I think it is also your responsibility to ensure that hiring managers and interviewers are aware of and adhere to the laws that govern the interview process.

As a trainer, I'd often play a quick game of "Legal Bingo", getting the participants to guess whether a practice was legal or not. I never had a class of hiring managers, interviewers or even recruiters that got it right. Most people, despite the video they're required to view when starting a new job, don't know the basic laws surrounding recruiting, and are likely putting your company in jeopardy by asking illegal questions or making illegal assumptions when asked to interview or make decisions about candidates.

The interviewers and recruiters had the most trouble with questions that sit on the fence – questions about favorite books, or college selection, for example. The questions themselves aren't illegal, but can lead to questionable discussions and, in court, keep in mind that employers can be held liable for such discussions, even if the candidate raises the topic. For example, a simple question, such as "What books have you read lately?" may lead the candidate to answer, "the Bible". At that point, the interviewer must skillfully redirect the conversation, or they may find themselves in trouble for making a decision about a candidate based on religion. Even though the candidate brought it up.

It's worthwhile to host a quarterly training that covers what should and shouldn't be asked during an interview. Even if you offer the 1-hour online course. Invite all interviewers to a short and fun lunch-and-learn to keep your interviewers up to date.

Selection discrimination is still persistent today. It is our job, as recruiting leaders, to root out discrimination by creating a process that is fair and that does not play into deliberate and unconscious bias. So that is the first thing we must do, examine and standardize our recruiting approach, weeding out practices that lend themselves to unfair, biased selection. In my opinion, the greatest risk here are the practices of not setting selection criteria in advance, unfair resume reviews and not thoroughly interviewing referred candidates. This is where I've seen organizations get into trouble – but all areas that can be easily fixed. As the TA leader, it is your job to ensure that senior leadership backs your efforts to embed practices that lead to unbiased, or de-biased selection of the best talent available to your organization.

Chapter 19 - End Notes

As we embark on a new journey to incorporate machine learning and artificial intelligence into every facet of recruiting, it is important to remember why we, recruiters, are here.

Industry pundits have described a world in which ML and AI will automate all of recruiting – that everything from sourcing, to interviewing, to assessing candidates, to recommending the optimal salary to compiling job offers can be handled by a computer. This may well be true for some organizations. Especially those companies with deep pockets and reliable access to internal and external data and the tech talent to take advantage of data riches. I dream of a system that can index every human mentioned on the internet, automatically categorizing them as likely or unlikely to consider positions within my org. The system would tag those who have already interacted with our TA systems and, with a few inputs, would bring up a list of candidates for our open positions, tagging them with a likelihood to accept an offer score. I won't hold my breath.

Despite automation and technology, hiring managers need the help of recruiters. They need us to activate systems, where available, and to tackle tasks manually where systems are inadequate or unavailable. Most importantly, recruiters are needed to drive decision-making and keep an eye on the fairness and integrity of that decision making. Recruiters play a critical role in exposing managers to a wide range of top candidates and helping managers decide how to build their teams. A well-developed recruiting organization can help organizations realize the teams needed to drive business success.

I'll leave you with one final story. Perhaps my crowning achievement as a recruiter. Remember the sales leader with whom I worked to deliver interview training after they offended a candidate to the extent that she called me? Well, that leader and I worked well together from the beginning. I was his recruiter.

In fact, I had inherited the search after it had been all but abandoned by another recruiter. I was new to the team. In fact, I was a brand-new manager, and I heard the plea to get the role filled. I reviewed the files – there were quite a few people who had been interviewed and rejected. The role was a Sales VP for the yet to be named AWS department. I reviewed the file and the candidates closely, preparing for the 10 minutes I'd get with the Senior VP to discuss the search. I didn't know the SVP very well, so I would have to ask the right questions quickly to better understand what I was up against. I went through all of the rejected candidates and tried to narrow down what they were looking for – and what wouldn't work. I got through my ten minutes with the leader, got a better understanding of what the leader wanted but I had little confidence that I could bring them what they needed.

They were looking for someone who could lead a growing sales team for a new tech product, that a) wouldn't be on the market for quite some time and b) was technically complex and unproven in the general market. I went about the job of sourcing, getting our agency involved and I returned to one of the candidates in the rejection pile. Out of curiosity, I called him. We talked for some time, and I thought, we might have passed over the best candidate for the role. It took a bit of work, but I convinced the leaders to spend more time with this candidate. "Why should we spend more time with him?" the CTO asked.

"Because he's asking questions. Tons of questions, that I can't answer. That maybe you can't answer. But they are the right questions."

So I asked the candidate to submit to a few more phone interviews, after which he became increasingly excited. He was excited about this new technology. We flew him in for interviews and after a lot of discussion (including plenty of exec conversations to which I was not privy), made him an offer. He was a tough negotiator. His stock package had to be included in the annual report. But he said yes.

On his first day, he found me to say thank you. I laughed and told him that he might feel differently in a few months. No, he told me. He was serious. The company he'd just left was on its last leg. (This was common knowledge. I was impressed that he was able to make his sales quota despite the dire position of the company). This job meant the world to him and *to his family.* I never forgot that. That what we do is often one of the most important things to ever happen to a person, to their families. That the decisions we drive are, in the end, *personal.*

He went on to build out a great sales team for Amazon's best-selling product. AWS grew to become a more than billion-dollar business. Eventually he left Amazon and hung a 'gone fishing' sign on his LinkedIn profile (literally). His hard bargaining led him to become a wealthy man. His hard work helped AWS become the largest cloud computing platform. I still feel honored to have been even remotely connected to making this happen.

As recruiters, that's what we have the privilege to do. If ever you're not excited to do this, to introduce people to perhaps their next greatest opportunity, then it's likely time to get out of this business. Recruiting can be difficult. Hiring managers can be demanding and candidates can be flaky and an ATS system can lose all the data you input. Talent competitors make better offers. The recruiter on the other team that just stole your best candidate. But nothing beats getting it right and making a hire. Nothing beats the hiring manager high fiving you in the break room because you delivered the perfect candidate. The candidate who brings you a handwritten card and a box of candy on their first day. Working with your recruiter buddy to pull off a recruiting blitz.

I love being a part of it! The ability to match people to the right opportunity at the right time is a gift. To endure the heartbreak when it doesn't work out. To get to a satisfying ending where the candidate, the hiring manager and the organization all get to thrive is the end goal. And I've been incredibly fortunate to, on occasion, help managers, candidates and companies get there.

Appendix

1. The Talent Board CandE Research Report

https://www.thetalentboard.org/benchmark-research/cande-research-reports/

2. Email to manager before the kickoff meeting

TO: Hiring Manager
CC: HR Business Partner
I'm the Recruiter for [focus area/department], and we will be partnering together to fill your open [title] position. I've sent an invite for a meeting where we will…

- Discuss your organization and how this role fits into your team and your priorities
- Discuss your target candidate profile (target companies, skills, competencies, etc.) and the target compensation package for this role
- Discuss our approach to finding and selling candidates
- Discuss our approach to assessing candidates, including people who will help you interview
- Outline the process, roles, and timelines for this recruiting effort

Please prepare for this meeting by…

- Bringing information about the team this person would work with (org chart, team mission/goals, location, etc)
- Bringing information about key people you may know who may be interested in this position, or who may be sources of referrals
- Identifying the key competencies and technical/functional, job specific skills that will be most critical for this hire to be successful [link to competencies and interview training on Intranet]
- Identifying the people (primary and alternates) who will be part of the interviewing process, including peers and key stakeholders

If you already have an internal employee or contractor who is an ideal candidate for this role, please bring relevant information to our meeting. I will prepare for our meeting by reviewing the job posting you submitted, researching the success of prior recruiting strategies for this kind of position, and creating a draft candidate generation and assessment plan. [I will/will not wait to post your position internally and externally.]

Thank you! I look forward to partnering with you on this search.
Best regards,
Name
Senior Recruiter
Focus Area

3. **Email to manager after the kickoff meeting**
   Subject Line: Our Recruitment Strategy: [title of position]. Please reply.

   Hello [Hiring Leader]
   TO: Hiring Manager
   CC: HR Business Partner, Recruiting Coordinator
   Thanks for your time [yesterday]. I look forward to partnering with you on this search and making a great hire. Please review the information below and reply to confirm our approach.

   Finding you the right candidate
   Based on our conversation about your target candidate profile, our plan to find someone, and prior successes filling this type of position, I expect we'll find your candidate by focusing our sourcing efforts on X and Y [X and Y = internal candidates, employee referrals, networking/direct sourcing, LinkedIn ads, etc. – pick top 2-3 sources].

   The Job Posting [Include this section only if position description needed an update after the strategy meeting]
   I have updated the job posting/advertisement to reflect the [additional/changed job responsibilities, requirements, selling points] we discussed. Please see the updated, attached posting and reply to confirm that it's accurate.

Target Compensation

We agreed that a target base salary of [XX,000 – YY,000] is appropriate for this role, which is a Level X. The bonus opportunity is Y, and this position is/is not approved for a sign-on bonus and/or relocation.

My Sourcing Action Items

Your position has already been posted to our careers site and [job board, other niche site]. To maximize X and Y, I'm going to [actions] by [tomorrow/the end of this week].

Your Sourcing Action Items

Also, since you also have sources we want to leverage, you agreed to [action] by [tomorrow/the end of this week]. Please be sure to pass along any leads or candidates you generate directly to me via email.

Screening and interviewing candidates

I will screen candidates as we find them and then pass them to you to complete the Hiring Manager screen [or have them scheduled directly on your calendar for 30-minute phone screens if [criteria]]. We will target a total of [3-5] qualified, diverse candidates for you interview. We agreed that [name] will act as your proxy should you be unavailable to screen a candidate.

- You'll be able to access resumes/candidates here: [link to ATS instructions for HMs]
- Once you screen a candidate, send me your feedback and we will either schedule an onsite interview or decline the candidate. It's critical that I receive your feedback within [X days].
- If we bring someone onsite, we will leverage the interview plan and interviewers outlined in the attachment to this email
- If you have scheduling support: [RC Name] is the primary Recruiting Coordinator who will be working closely with me and scheduling interviews for this role

Onsite interviews

Per our discussion, we will bring candidates who pass your phone screen onsite to meet with the following interviewers who will each focus on a different skill or performance area. We agreed that we will target no more than [4, 5] interviewers TOTAL for each candidate.

Role	Primary Names	Alternate Names	Focus Areas (i.e. Skills and Experience/ Accomplishments, Compentencies, Demo/ Case Study)	Time Needed
Hiring Manager (HM)		HM or Proxy must be on every interview loop		
Peer (s)				
Stakeholder(s)				
HM's Director/ VP?				

Interviewing Best Practices: Please refer to our Interviewing Training Materials [link to training and guides] for details on how to best evaluate a candidate against our core hiring criteria and your job-specific hiring criteria.

Our planned timelines

Given the recruiting process we agreed to and our typical time to fill metrics for this type of position, I expect we'll **hold onsite interviews the week of W and select our finalist by the week of W+2. Given the typical [3-4 day] offer approval process, and a typical [2-12] week notice period, I expect we'll fill this position as soon as the week of W+7-15.** Of course, we'll both do everything we can to accelerate this process while maintaining a great candidate experience and high hiring bar.

Please let me know if you have any questions about anything related to this search. I'm here to help and look forward to partnering with you on this search.

Thank you!

4. **Sourcing books.** Following are my favorites, in no particular order. There are plenty others out there, all worthwhile to check out. Find the books, websites, and resources that speak to you. I tend to rely on resources that help me with tech recruiting, but most of these are filled with tips that are helpful to all recruiters and sourcers:

    a. *Talk Tech to Me, Brian Fink* – Thorough, filled with easy explanations, including a nice primer on Boolean search.

    b. *The Non-Technical Guide to Web Technologies* – Dated survey of technology (written in 2013) but easy to understand and brief. With drawings. A must for tech recruiters.

    c. *Technology Made Simple for the Technical Recruiter, Obi Ogbanufe* – A thorough guide for tech recruiters (the shorter, updated version is best)

    d. *The Talent Sourcing & Recruiting Handbook, by Shally Steckerl* – A thorough primer on sourcing tactics. A bit expensive, but worth it.

5. **LinkedIn Job Description Heat Map**
   https://www.linkedin.com/business/talent/blog/talent-acquisition/job-description-heatmap

6. Candidate Submittal email

Subject Line: Bobbi Lakeman, Date, Company, Great candidate for your [job title] role – reply by tomorrow 6pm

Hello [Hiring Manager]

I will schedule him for a call with you for Tuesday unless I hear back from you by tomorrow 6pm that you are not interested. This is a great candidate, who will not stay on the market long.

Name: Bobbi Lakeman
Companies: Senior Product Manager at Salesforce (current, for 3 years), [Role] at ABC (prior, for X years), [Role] at DEF (prior, for X years)
Experience Match: Has project managed X, led Y, deployed Z
Technical Match: Achieved X using [technical skills, technologies, languages you want], self rates [technology/technical skills] as 8/10, tested in [technology/technical skills] as 8/10
Fit: strong pm skills, has continuously worked to update his skills, was able to handily explain the technical aspects of his projects, struggles with his current manager who is a micro-manager", great example of leading developing and implementing solutions in the field of X, understands his business/customer very well
Motivators: Wants to [gain experience doing X, build Y, scale Z, lead A]. Would only make a move if...
Compensation: We can afford her. Current XXX,000 base, YY,000 annual bonus (paid out every [month]). No stock options. Will not make a move for less than [comp], which is within our range.
Relocation: She's local. Commutes to [city] now, so we'd be about 15 minutes closer. Prefers telecommuting when possible.
Timing: Has an interview with [competitor] scheduled for next Friday. Wants to make a move after bonus is paid out in [month] [or is interested in having a position finalized by X date].
Next Steps: Phone Screen and Sell by you, next Tuesday (he's open between 4-7pm). Wants to learn more about the ABC project and the team's priorities for this year and

the future. You'll want to dig into his experience with [programs, projects, or assignments] and get a sense for the scale of the X projects he led. If we decide to bring him in, he can get away for an onsite interview a week from Monday.

I will schedule him for a call with you for Tuesday unless I hear back from you by tomorrow 6pm that you are not interested.

Resume Attached, LinkedIn Link, Blog Link

Thanks!

Name
Recruiter, Focus Area

7. Candidate Outreach Email Example

Subject: Liza – Data Science Opportunity –at MyCompany

Liza – My CTO, Penny, and I were reviewing some of the work you've talked about on [site]. You have an impressive background in XYZ. Here at MyCompany, we're doing some early-stage work around XYZ that we think will change the way consumers do LMNOP.

The team has less than 10 people on it now, but the work will ultimately touch hundreds of millions of people. Would you be interested in learning more about what we're doing?

Please reply to this email or use my online calendar to schedule a brief chat at your convenience.

I look forward to our conversation!

End Notes

I'd like to offer a huge trough of gratitude to all the people in the industry that informed and polished my approach to talent acquisition. There are so many to name. I'll start with Sarah and Jeanine – my Amazon homies. We learned so much together. Thank you for taking me seriously when it mattered and ignoring me when I was wrong! You continue to inspire me.

I'd also like to shout out Beth and Brandie, both amazing TA leaders. Thank you for reading through this and offering your suggestions! And thanks for being my sounding board! And shout out to Jackie too!

Going even further back in my professional history, I'd like to thank Marla, who shepherded me into my very first recruiting role at Egon Zendher International.

And there are many, many others who deserve my unwavering gratitude. For showing me how to do it just a little better. For giving me room to experiment. For sharing in the pure joy of getting it right. For shielding me from the results of some error I made. I mentioned some of the leadership from those early days at Amazon, but I wouldn't want to forget folks like Jim Bisbee, Barbie Winterbottom, Shoma Chatterjee, Margo Wheeler, Christine Deputy, Carol Mahoney, Nina Johal, Robin Andrulevich, Deb Hester and many, many others. I don't want to forget my colleagues and clients at Recruiting Toolbox, with whom I have had hours of conversation about how to recruit better. To John, Ben, Matt, Paul, Alecia, Annie and a few former Toolboxers, you were and remain daily inspiration for me.

Lastly, there are a few folks in my life who have definitely crossed the line from professional to friendships, for which I am extremely grateful. These folks are always in my corner, always available for a quick check-in, always good for solid, sage advice, and they, like me, don't take everything so seriously. To Alecia, Chris, Chris, Eric, Jon, Lisa, Jenny, Mark, Ryan, Nancy, and Teela, thank you from the bottom of my heart!

Made in the USA
Coppell, TX
09 April 2024

31080201R10087